The Prayer
of the
Presence of God

Dom Augustin Guillerand

The Prayer
of the
Presence of God

SOPHIA INSTITUTE PRESS®
Manchester, New Hampshire

The Prayer of the Presence of God, a 1965 translation of *Face à Dieu* (Rome: Benedictines of St. Priscilla, 1956), was formerly published in English in 1965 by Dimension Books, Wilkes-Barre, Pennsylvania. This 2005 edition by Sophia Institute Press® contains minor editorial revisions.

Cover design by Theodore Schluenderfritz

On the cover: Painted Cross, by Meo da Siena; image Copyright © Arte & Immagini srl/CORBIS

Sophia Institute Press®
Box 5284, Manchester, NH 03108
1-800-888-9344
www.sophiainstitute.com

Imprimi potest: Fr. Ferdinand, Prior Cartusiae,
In domo Cartusiae, March 19, 1965
Imprimatur: Cyrillus Episcopus, Southwarcensis
April 27, 1966

Library of Congress Cataloging-in-Publication Data

Guillerand, Augustin, 1877-1945.
   [Face à Dieu. English]
   The prayer of the presence of God / Augustin Guillerand.
      p. cm.
   Includes bibliographical references.
   ISBN 1-933184-12-4 (pbk. : alk. paper)
   1. Prayer — Christianity. 2. Meditation — Christianity.
I. Title.
   BV4813.G813 2005
   248.3′2 — dc22   2005025795

Day after day, O Lord of my life,
shall I stand before Thee, face-to-face.

With folded hands, O Lord of all worlds,
shall I stand before Thee, face-to-face.

Under the great sky, in solitude
and silence, with humble heart,
shall I stand before Thee, face-to-face.

Rabindranath Tagore

Contents

Foreword xi

Part 1
True Prayer

1. Turn toward God in prayer 5
2. Rely on prayer as your soul's defense 9
3. Recognize your dependence on God 13
4. Pray for an awareness of sin's horror 17
5. Reflect continuously on the need to pray 19
6. Use forms of prayer that draw you toward God 23
7. Let prayer refresh your soul 27
8. Rejoice that God answers prayers 31
9. Ask for God alone 35
10. Assist your prayer with various means 39
11. Practice almsgiving and humility 41

Part 2
Perfecting Your Prayer

12. Detach yourself from earthly things 47
13. Unite your will with God's 49

14. Revere God. 51

15. Pray with attention 55

16. Guard your heart 57

17. Place yourself in God's presence 59

18. Persevere in prayer 61

19. Have confidence in God. 63

20. Understand why God makes you wait. 65

21. Pray with persistence 67

22. Avoid lengthy prayers 69

23. Ponder God's greatness. 73

24. Understand the power of humility 75

25. Pray with your heart 79

26. Be sorry for your sins 83

27. Reflect on what Christ suffered because of sin. 87

Part 3

Growing Closer to God

28. Prepare yourself to pray 91

29. Enter your "inner chamber". 95

30. Rejoice in God's attentiveness to you 99

31. Let prayer bring peace to your soul 103

32. Develop a filial relationship with God. 107

33. Meet God in the silence of your soul. 111

34. Speak to God as a child to his father. 115

35. Remember that God acts for your good 119

36. Strive for a proper attitude of soul 121

37. Persist in prayer when God seems absent 127

Part 4

The Prayer of Praise

38. Let your praise be a foretaste of eternity 133

39. Praise of man's powerlessness 135

40. Praise of God's goodness 137

41. Praise of God's wisdom 139

42. Praise of God's truth. 143

43. Praise of God's mercy 147

44. Praise of God's justice. 153

45. Praise of God's life. 155

46. Praise of all the divine perfections 161

47. Praise of creation. 165

꩜

Biographical Note: Dom Augustin Guillerand 169

Foreword

The following pages are a translation of *Face à Dieu*, by the Carthusian Dom Augustin Guillerand. It is perhaps necessary to explain that, like the rest of Dom Guillerand's writings, this particular work was not written as a book or indeed even in chapter form, but consists of jottings made at various times as the ideas occurred to him, mostly in the course of his meditations on the divine truths. In most cases, it is true — and in the case of this work it is certainly true — there is a more or less formal sequence of thought throughout the work. But the subject is so vast and so profound that it is inevitable that, without the most careful and prolonged revision, the work (whether in the original or in this translation) is bound to lack the unity and orderly presentation we would expect in a treatise of this nature. Whether the author ever intended to make such a revision we do not know. In any case, his death in April 1945 at the Grande Chartreuse made such a revision impossible, so far as he was concerned.

It was only after his death that these notes were discovered, put into order by a monk of a Charterhouse in France, and published by the Benedictines of St. Priscilla in Rome in 1956.

Such being the case, this work is bound to present in some senses the appearance of an unfinished production, and at first reading it might seem as if many of the ideas are repeated unnecessarily. To a certain extent this is true; but, even so, we venture to think that the author's treatment of the subject will bear, and even gain by, such repetitions, and that very often a second reading will reveal depths and still greater depths as a result of the reiteration of the author's thought.

After all, the subject of these meditations is prayer, from its obvious meaning to its highest implications, and Dom Guillerand's treatment of it was not meant to be either a formal theological treatise or a work of popularization. In fact, it is nothing other than a record of his thoughts as he penetrated — as he could penetrate — more and more deeply into a subject that is beyond depth. One of the joys of this author's writings is that, with every fresh reading, we always see further and deeper into realms of awe and beauty hitherto unsuspected.

The Preface to the first French edition repeats that these lines were never, in the author's intention, meant to be read by others, much less published, but were simply an outward manifestation or record (a habit of the author's) of what was virtually a life of contemplation or a "long regard," as the author calls it elsewhere, "constantly renewed." His life was indeed one "long regard" of the divine realities, above all of what he calls "the great Reality": God.

As arranged in the text that follows, this work falls into four main parts, based on certain indications left by the author himself. The first part he calls "True Prayer," and it deals principally with the more rudimentary notions of prayer: its definition, its necessity, and its differing forms. So far as its definition is concerned, for Dom Augustin there is only essential prayer, and that is "the movement drawing the soul upward to God and away from self, and the relationship that follows." He insists, however, upon the necessity for the mind to do its part. "With prayer," he says, "it

Foreword

is not just a matter of having read and realized *for the moment* its grandeur, the immense blessings it confers, the glory it gives to God, and its mission in the world. We must return to these thoughts again and again; we must constantly reflect on them and *live* them. . . . We must continually look for the essential Beauty behind the external beauty of things. We must turn from the weakness of our fallen nature to the strong tenderness of the Son of God, who became our Redeemer and is ever ready to receive us back into his favor."

And even in these early pages, he introduces the first note of the theme that gradually occupies more and more the scope of his thought: the place of *praise* in essential prayer. "We were made," he says, "to praise God eternally. Hearing on our lips the exiles' song of the Fatherland, He knows that we want Him more than any created thing, and that we belong to Him completely." By this time, the soul has already made a considerable advance in prayer.

Lofty as is the author's approach to prayer in general, he never for long loses sight of the part played by God's creative works in a life of prayer. The soul is gradually being taught to see the reflection of the divine attributes in "the work of His hands." "During the hours of sleep," he continues, "the soul does not offer to God, who is still its all, the homage of the whole being for which it is responsible, but on awakening it resumes command and becomes once more the link and interpreter of the created world, thus renewing its conscious contact with its Creator. That is why at Lauds [he has in mind especially choir religious] we invite the whole of creation to take up again its interrupted praise: *All ye works of the Lord, bless the Lord; praise and exalt Him above all forever.* Thus sings the soul to all creation, and all creation responds as with one voice."

The Prayer of the Presence of God

The second part, "Perfecting Your Prayer" deals with the spirit of detachment as the indispensable condition for all prayer — not by any means detachment for its own sake, but in order that the soul may be set free for its ascent toward God, which is true prayer. Throughout the whole of this part — and indeed throughout the whole work — the author insists that prayer is impossible without the fundamental recognition that we are "nothing" and that God is all, and that man is utterly dependent on Him. Indeed, his favorite expression for the Almighty is *L'être*, or HE WHO IS, which, after all, is the only name God gave Himself in the beginning.[1] Then follow chapters on reverence, attention, the Guard of the heart, confidence and humility — chapters that again slowly trace the soul's ascent in prayer.

The title of the third part, "Growing Closer to God" is sufficiently indicative of the chapters contained in it. First, there is the preparation for this higher form of prayer, which the author describes as the entry into the soul's innermost chamber, where God, the Spirit of love, dwells. "But thou, when thou shalt pray, enter into thy chamber."[2] "God is a brazier of love, and in prayer we are drawn near to Him, and are caught by His fire." Here the soul is being drawn close to HIM WHO IS and who gives being to all things. Then follows a chapter on the divine friendship, as the relationship between the soul and God develops, and the soul is

---

[1] Cf. Exod. 3:13-14: "Moses said to God, 'Lo, I shall go to the children of Israel and say to them, "The God of your fathers hath sent me to you." If they shall say to me, "What is His name?" what shall I say to them?' God said to Moses, 'I AM WHO AM.' He said, 'Thus shalt thou say to the children of Israel: "HE WHO IS hath sent me to you." ' "

[2] Matt. 6:6.

introduced in prayer almost into the presence of the company of Heaven. "In such company we forget the earth, we become serene, consoled, and strong." And finally, the soul enters what our author calls significantly "the silent place." He does not neglect the trials through which the soul may have to pass, and in "Prayer's Sublime Moments," he describes how the soul is fortified by these trials (of darkness, abandonment, and so on) for a still higher form of prayer.

That higher form of prayer is dealt with in perhaps the most satisfactory part, the fourth and final part, which he calls "The Prayer of Praise."

Here we must confess we are immediately in deep waters. In successive chapters, our author describes — or attempts to describe — in wonderful language, admittedly at times a little difficult to follow, the inner life of the Blessed Trinity. But the point he is always attempting to bring out is that, as good as it is to adore God in the concrete examples of His goodness and other attributes, these are not, and never can be, "the boundless reality which is God Himself, who alone can satisfy the soul in its search for ultimate Truth. . . . In order to recognize the supreme order, we must pass beyond the duration of time and place and circumstances — in short, of what *is not* — and wait until the passing and superficial moment has produced what the eternal gaze sees and the supreme Love wills." He reminds us that all the divine perfections (for so we call them, since we can see them only in the broken mirror of His creative works) are in fact but the single perfection of His plenitude of being: a unity which *is* simplicity, which *is* life, which *is* love, which *is* truth.

Finally, he concludes — so as not to leave us, as it were, suspended in midair — by returning to the contemplation of God in His works, and this he calls "The Praise of Creation." It is a case of

The Prayer of the Presence of God

"In Thy light we shall see Light."[3] Having gazed — as we are told the eagle gazes unblinking at the sun — at the light itself of divine Truth unveiled (insofar as it can be perceived in this life), the soul returns to contemplate the divine Being reflected in His created works.

The author's final prayer is that, by the perfect gift of himself to God (which is what love is), he may give himself in all things and thus bring back to the divine Majesty the praise of all creation, spiritualized.

In laying down the book at this point, one is almost instinctively reminded of the words of another who, like our author, had the vision of a poet and the faith of a man of God:

> Ah! how the City of our God is fair.
> If, without sea and starless though it be:
> For joy of the majestic beauty there,
> Man shall not miss the stars nor mourn the sea.

St. Hugh's Charterhouse
Parkminster

---

[3] Ps. 35:10 (RSV = Ps. 36:9).

*The Prayer of
the Presence of God*

Part 1

True Prayer

Chapter 1

Turn toward God in prayer

St. John Damascene's[4] definition of prayer is well known. "Prayer," he says, "is asking God for what is fitting." We must probe this thought thoroughly, draw from the words their substance, separate its parts, and, having done so, restore them to the deep life of this substance which sustains them and gives them life.

This definition of prayer falls, then, into two parts, which are, as it were, its matter and form. Prayer is an asking, but an asking of God, and consequently bears the impress of Him to whom it is addressed. We can ask God only for what He wants us to ask of Him, and He can will only what is conformable to His will. Now, since God is one of the "terms" of prayer — that is, we pray *to* Him — and since He is infinite order, prayer is a request essentially "ordered," in other words, consonant with the order of God Himself. What is that order? It is what He is — Being Himself: that being from whom, by whom, and for whom all things *are*.[5] He is our beginning and our end.[6] He is the light of our mind and the strength of our will. He is truth, goodness, and beauty unalloyed, the source of all joy, and the ocean of all life.

---

[4] St. John Damascene (676-749), Greek theologian, orator, philosopher, Father, and Doctor.

[5] Cf. John 1:3; Col. 1:16.

[6] Cf. Apoc. 1:8 (RSV = Rev. 1:8).

The Prayer of the Presence of God

What is "fitting," therefore — what we must ask God for — is *Himself*; to be united with Him, to be transformed in Him; to possess Him and to be possessed by Him. We should ask to enter, by grace, into such intimate relations with Him as unite us to Him; to become His sons by a communication as complete as possible of His Spirit of love; to share in that joy and in that life which is His joy and His life — in short, to share in joy itself and life itself. The Scriptures are full of this prayer, which is constantly bubbling up like springs of water on a high mountain. "The Lord is the portion of my inheritance," says the psalmist.[7] "For what have I in Heaven, and besides Thee what do I desire upon earth? . . . Thou art the God of my heart, and my portion forever.[8]

In the case of the intelligent being, to possess is to see the object of one's love and to find one's complete happiness in it. What we see enters into us by an image, which makes the object present to us; we say expressly it "re-presents" it to us. This presence allows us to contemplate it, and that contemplation, in turn, engraves in us the features of what we see. Once engraved, these features are like a continual presence, which perpetually renews our joy.

There is another kind of knowledge and presence that brings neither possession nor pleasure. The object is within us, but it is not part of ourselves. We do not make use of it, nor have we any desire to profit by it. We are content with the image, but we experience no conscious need for any immediate, direct contact with the reality it represents. We do not love that object, for it is not our "good." We do not seek to be united with it, or to be transformed in it; we are content merely to know what it is and that it exists; but that knowledge awakens in us no desire for a more intimate

---

[7] Ps. 15:5 (RSV = Ps. 16:5).
[8] Ps. 72:25-26 (RSV = Ps. 73:25-26).

union with it, or for mutual self-surrender. We rightly love what is "good," but that object does not seem to be our good.

On the other hand, we recognize God as our supreme good, and we long for the closest union with Him, for the most complete possession, and consequently for that clear, direct vision which brings joy — an intuitive vision, a direct contact with His being giving Himself, to which we respond by the total gift of ourselves to His total gift of Himself. This is what we ask for before everything else, and anything else we ask for is ordered toward this. It cannot be otherwise, because the one has always the end in view, the other only the means to that end. Our whole purpose is to arrive at that end.

Now, there are two kinds of means that lead to this desired union. One clears the way of obstacles; the other puts us in touch with the object of our love. We pray to God to keep us from all that might separate us from Him or delay our union; at the same time, we ask for what will bring about that union. It is vices and sins that separate, temptations that can hold us up. To obtain the mastery of them, therefore, should be the first object of our prayer, and we must not make light of this. Those who are proud or only (more often) simple and inexperienced, content themselves with asking for union; many, indeed, try to live that union immediately. It does not occur to them that there is danger here. The enemy's blows, they say, cannot touch them. They consider themselves immune, whereas they are simply ignorant and blind. It would be an exaggeration to say that they are endangering their salvation, but they are very much exposed to mark time, and to become paralyzed.

The first act of light is to be separated from darkness,[9] and to light up all that it touches. It shines and is visible; it lights up the

---

[9] Cf. Gen. 1:4: "[God] divided the light from the darkness."

way and the end only insofar as it separates itself and the other objects from the night. When it emerges from the darkness and wrests a soul from it, the light reveals to that soul the love that has given it being and action. It is now that the Holy Spirit makes His power felt. He draws the soul to Himself and awakens a reciprocal movement toward union. He causes virtues to flourish in the soul, communicating His own dispositions to it, and becomes the hidden cause of all its activity. He prays in it, adores in it, utters cries of love, and pours Himself forth in the most wonderful colloquies and unspeakable groanings,[10] repeating unceasingly, "Abba, Father."[11]

St. Augustine's[12] definition of prayer suggests the same thought. "Prayer is a devout movement of the soul toward God," he says, thus putting into words what must have been most certainly his own form of prayer. In all movement there are two terms: the one from which we set out, the other toward which we tend. When we pray, one of the terms does not exist: it is "nothingness," or rather it is a being who exists solely by Him toward whom it tends. To let our gaze, therefore, rest on this nothingness as on an end is foolish. By not looking at ourselves, we are by that very fact continually moving in the direction of our true end, which is God, and our prayer is continuous and one that realizes our divine Master's command to pray always.[13]

---

[10] Rom. 8:26.
[11] Rom. 8:15; Gal. 4:6.
[12] St. Augustine (354-430), Bishop of Hippo.
[13] Luke 18:1.

Chapter 2

⌒

Rely on prayer as your soul's defense

Prayer is the duty of every moment. We ought always to pray, said our Lord.[14] And what He said, He did; therein lay His great power. Action accompanied His words and corresponded with them. We must pray always in order to be on our guard.[15] Our life, both of body and soul, our natural and supernatural life, is like a fragile flower. We live surrounded by enemies. Ever since man rejected the Light that was meant to show him the way,[16] everything has become for us an obstacle and a danger; we live in the shadow of death.[17] Instead of pointing to the Creator and leading us to Him, things show only themselves, with the result that we stop at them. The Devil, to whom we stupidly gave them when we gave him ourselves, speaks to us through their many voices; his shadow darkens their transparence. Beyond their attractive forms we no longer seek the beauty they reflect, but merely the pleasure and satisfaction they are able to offer us.

But the enemy is not only at our door; he is even more within us. And he is at our door, because he is within us. It is we who have

---

[14] Luke 18:1.
[15] Matt. 26:41.
[16] John 1:5.
[17] Luke 1:79; Ps. 106:10 (RSV = Ps. 107:10).

invited him in. In turning toward him, we have turned the whole universe away from God. This is why the world is against us. It is inimical, hostile to us, and not without reason. Through the world and by it, we have let war loose within ourselves and in everything. This is only what we would expect, but it is terrible all the same.

What a profound definition of peace is St. Augustine's! Above all, in these days, when the world is convulsed to its center,[18] when men and things (the latter through men) serve only to kill and destroy, how necessary it is to ponder well these words, whose very sound is full of the calm they express: *Peace is the tranquillity of order.* Order means that everything is in its proper place. God made men superior to all things,[19] and all things turned to God as to their source, to receive from Him their being moment by moment, and to thank Him and bless Him. That was the way God acted, and this is His order and His peace. It was this that fundamentally constituted the terrestrial paradise, and will one day be the heavenly Paradise for those who have understood and taken up again this attitude.

⌒

I remember seeing once a frightened and hunted animal that had lost its way. It rushed through an open gate that led into a garden full of flowers, with what disastrous results can be imagined. This is an image, although a very imperfect one, of a soul when it allows the wild beast of the world to enter into it, ever since our first parents turned away from God and listened to the voice of the

[18] These words were written during the second World War.
— TRANS.
[19] Cf. Gen. 2:15.

Tempter. As a consequence, we live in a country occupied by the enemy, and it is our business to drive him out of it; to turn away from him and turn back to God, and so secure our liberty. And we have to do this without any armed or organized forces; with our faculties in disorder, our strength impaired, and surrounded by enemies on all sides or by those who are indifferent to our lot. No greater helplessness could be imagined, had we not God.

And that is why prayer is so necessary, and why our Lord had to tell us so insistently to pray, and to pray always. Hence, too, His saying which can seem so overwhelming: "Without me, you can do nothing,"[20] as well as His invitation so consoling and comforting: "Come to me. . . ."[21]

Prayer is the soul's response to that invitation. It comes; it makes known its wretchedness, it pleads for help, for light for the mind and strength for the will. It asks for grace to bring its passions under the control of its higher will, and to submit that will to God, who is order and peace. And God says to the soul, "I am and always will be a Father. I love you and await your coming. . . . Come!" And the soul replies, "My God, I can do no more. Come to me."

[20] John 15:5.
[21] Matt. 11:28.

Chapter 3

≈

Recognize your dependence on God

The reasons for praying are as numerous as they are imperative. They correspond to all our needs without exception, and to all occasions. They are also in accord with the favors we receive in answer to our prayers and to God's rights over His creatures.

Our divine Master's word has explored and lighted up everything, our human world and God's world. He revealed the powerlessness of the first when he said, "Without me, you can do nothing."

We have read these words often enough, but without penetrating them. We no more understand the "nothing" than we do the "All." The nature of our being does not allow us to understand it. We do not look at our tiny being as it actually is in the light of the All. We do not compare the hours of our life, so short and transient, with God's changeless eternity. We do not see the place we occupy in the universe as compared with His immensity, which infinitely overflows our tiny universe, and could embrace numberless others, far greater than ours.

Above all, we forget that our being is not ours. Moment by moment we receive the tiny drop of being that God deigns to give us. The only reason we have it is because He gives it to us; and having received it, immediately it begins to dissolve; it slips through our fingers and is replaced by another, which escapes us with the same rapidity. All this being comes from God and returns to Him; it depends upon Him alone. We are like vessels into which He pours that being, drop by drop, so as to create a bond of dependence upon Him, whereby His being is manifested and made known and, when lovingly welcomed, is glorified.

Prayer is this intelligent vessel, which knows, loves, thanks, and glorifies. It says, in effect:

> *My God, the present moment*
> *and the light by which I am aware of it,*
> *comes from You. My mind, which appreciates it;*
> *the upward leaping of my heart, which responds*
> *to that recognition and thanks You for it;*
> *the living bond created by this moment — all is from You.*
> *Everything comes from You.*
> *All that is within me, all that is not You;*
> *all created beings and their movements;*
> *my whole being and its activities — all is from You.*
> *Without You nothing exists; apart from You is just nothingness;*
> *apart from Your being there is merely nonexistence.*

How this complete dependence, upon which I have so often and so deeply meditated, ought to impress me! I feel that it plunges me into the depths of reality, into truth. Nevertheless, it does not completely express that reality. There was a time when this nothingness rose up in opposition to HIM WHO IS. It wanted to be independent of Him; it put itself forward, refused to obey Him, and cut itself off from Him. It made war on Him and became His enemy. It destroyed His image in the heart's citadel, where hitherto He had reigned, and usurped His throne.

These are only metaphors, and they do not do justice to the real horror of the plight created by sin; but we must be content with them, as they are all we have. We must remember, however, that they are completely inadequate. And every day we add to this predicament, already so grave. Every personal sin of ours is an acceptance of this state: we choose it; we love it and prefer it to union with God. We lap up, as it were, these sins like water. We take pleasure in plunging into them as into a stream whose waters rise persistently and in time overwhelm us and carry us away. They toss us about like a straw and submerge us. Thoughts, feelings, words, really bad acts, and innumerable omissions fill our days and nights, and intermingle, more or less consciously, with our every movement, and at all hours. They spoil the purity of our ordinary actions such as eating and drinking; they introduce themselves into our sleep and mix with our waking movements, and with our external acts as with our most intimate thoughts. Because of our fallen state, everything becomes matter and occasion to drag us down further into evil.

Chapter 4

⪰

Pray for an awareness of sin's horror

There is in the soul of man a fire of concupiscence constantly burning, inherited from our first parents. It spreads its noxious heat to the soul's powers; it gives rise to sensuality in the flesh under a thousand varying forms; to error and illusion in the mind, so that we mistake what *is not* for the God *who is*. It causes us to seek as our good what in fact draws us away from it, while the will finds itself drawn to the transient pleasures offered us by our senses, leaving us powerless to follow its deeper urge to seek its true spiritual good.

In the course of time, successive generations have greatly increased these tendencies, while our personal sins add to the burden daily. As a result, our whole being has been reduced to a state of disorder and anarchy, from which we continue to suffer so long as we retain any sense of order and discipline. We can unfortunately end up by becoming more or less accustomed to this state of affairs, and this is the worst misery of all.

We walk on a downward and dangerous slope, and have done so ever since we were born. All our energies are inclined toward evil, and are drawn by it. Our mind is distorted and no longer faithfully reflects the truth. All too readily, ignorance, the love of falsehood, and vain curiosities find a welcome in it. Our will is weakened and no longer takes command. Badly enlightened by the mind enticing it in wrong directions, and carried away by unchecked passions inflamed by external objects, at every moment it is mastered by servants who have ceased to obey, if they have not actually gone so far as to subject the will entirely to their caprices.

What hope is there for us without help from on high, opposing its higher movement to this lower movement? We must pray, therefore, for this aid that we need so badly; for the forgiveness of our sins, and for that true contrition which blots them out. We must pray for the graces of expiation which offers all the reparation of which we are capable, and for that charity which gives us new life. We must have the courage to welcome that divine light which shows up our sins, more numerous than the sands of the shore, weighing us down with their load and crushing us like the suffocating air that presages a storm. Like the snows of an avalanche and the rocks they bring with them, our sins pile up one on the other, erecting a barrier between our soul and Heaven, until we forget that there is a Heaven at all! We must pray that we may realize all the horror of one single sin, and the great number of which we have been guilty. We must ask for that frightening light which reveals them all — the sins we have committed knowingly and those, far more numerous, that we have committed almost unconsciously, just as we take in the germs that fill the air we breathe.

⌒

Chapter 5

Reflect continuously on the need to pray

The saints and spiritual writers constantly return to this idea of the disorder within us, which is the consequence of sin, and they are right to do so. Like them, I repeat: Life is not literature. Before we can assimilate anything, we have to turn it over in our minds again and again. To take in and to assimilate is a slow process. The mind has to concentrate on its object for a long time, if it is to take on its form and live it.

This object is a positive one: it is God, the ideal form and the perfect model. But it is also, on the other hand, all that is opposed to His pure image and to His communication of life. God wants to transform us into sons of light, but He finds us children of darkness. He wants His Spirit, the Spirit of love, who is the gift of self, to live in us, but He finds us possessed by another spirit that is the love of self. This negative element, which surrounds us only after a struggle, must disappear.

Life is a battle, a battle between God and the spirit of evil. When a soul ceases to fight, it may be counted as hopelessly lost. And a soul that does not pray is one that has given in without a struggle. It possesses a kind of peace, but it is the peace of an occupied territory, conquered by the invader and resigned to his domination.

What we find blameworthy in spiritual writers is not that they insist on this too much, but that they do not insist on it enough.

The Prayer of the Presence of God

We are living in an age of knowledge rather than of understanding. Pure reasoning and memory hold the day. The whole object of so much of our writing is to satisfy these cravings, to provide men with ideas rather than to enrich their souls and deepen their lives. It is the fashion today to write popular works and articles in magazines for people living in the world. They must know everything and be able to talk about the latest book or the most recent discovery. Men's minds are like those artificial floral displays we see on festive occasions. We arrange beautiful flowers, which we enjoy without having cultivated them. We do not even know their names, and by the morrow we have forgotten all about them.

With prayer it is not just a matter of having read and realized for the moment its necessity, its grandeur, the immense blessings it confers, its increasing comfort, the glory it gives to God and its mission to the world. We must return to these thoughts again and again; we must constantly reflect on them and live them. This is what the Holy Spirit does in the Scriptures, what the Church does in its offices, and what the saints do in their daily prayers and constant meditations. We must continually look for the essential beauty behind the external beauty of things. We must turn from the weakness of our fallen nature to the strong tenderness of the Son of God, who became our Redeemer and is ever ready to receive us back into His favor. We must turn from the perpetual menace of the Devil and of the world that hangs over us, to the unfailing help that is offered us by our Savior, whose great desire is to rescue us from their tyranny.

Our principal danger is a spiritual one: the danger of losing our true life; all other dangers are directed toward this. They are the various ways in which each of us may be put to the test. We must pray, therefore, before all else, that God may live in us and we in Him. We must pray that our trials may contribute to that divine life, which is the only true life and the only true good. We may ask that God will, in His goodness, preserve us from persecutions, injustices, calumnies, attacks of one kind and another on our interests and rights, illnesses of body and mind — but always subject to the designs of His love, which must be our chief rule in all we ask for.

In His loving plan, God has foreseen that we must be tested, but He knows also that the patience with which we bear such trials in union with our divine Lord can prove an exceptionally rich and pure source of merit and of grace to expiate our sins. He knows that our natural and supernatural growth (the latter bringing the former within its scope) will in general be proportioned to such trials, and that the divine image, the reflection of the model of infinite beauty, will shine resplendent in us as a result of these trials. In spite of myself, I return to these thoughts again and again; they do not exclude others, but they seem to me to embrace and assimilate them.

Chapter 6

⌒

Use forms of prayer
that draw you toward God

There is only one essential prayer: it is the movement drawing the
soul upward toward God, and the relationship that follows. As
soon as the soul turns from the dark valley to the heights where
there is light and gladness, it prays. It meets Him who has never
been absent and who is always turned toward the soul, His hands
full of blessings, His heart overflowing with eternal love, and the
relationship that is love and life begins.

This relationship can assume very different forms, which vary
according to persons, times, needs, and with the varying circumstances of everyday life.

There are times when we find comfort in the thought of God's
greatness in general, or in some particular perfection of His. For
instance, we invoke His love, His mercy, His goodness, His holiness, and His truth. These perfections serve to raise us to the contemplation of those vast horizons where the God who *is* becomes
ever greater in our eyes. We do well. God has only Himself. He
cannot resist such praise. We were made for that: to praise Him
eternally. Hearing on our lips this exiles' song of the Fatherland, He knows that we want Him more than any created thing,
and that we belong to Him completely. The Scriptures are full of
this prayer. "O my God, hear me," cries David, "for Thou art all

goodness and mercy."[22] And Daniel: "O Lord, hear [and] be appeased: hearken and do. Delay not for Thy own sake."[23]

Often we turn to someone dear to the divine Majesty. Obviously our Lord's sacred humanity occupies the very first place, far above everyone and everything. In this respect the litanies of the saints are wonderful. We first invoke God Himself, then Jesus, His Mother, the great saints of our immense and loving family in Heaven. Then we recall the difficulties of the way and the dangers that threaten us, and finally, gathering it all up into an immense and powerful *finale*, we recall the main details of all that our Redeemer has done for us in giving Himself to us. We end on a note of supplication, on our own behalf and for others, for the souls in Purgatory as well as for those who are still on earth: "We beseech Thee, O Lord. . . ."

The diversity of our requests also imparts to our prayer an infinite variety of shades. We can ask for the absolute good, which is God Himself, and for the eventual possession of this supreme good. We can ask for the means that lead us to Him. Among these means, some are directly and essentially directed to that end, others less so. Our prayer varies according to these objects. There is the prayer that consists solely of praise and adoration; another restricts itself to thanksgiving. But all are essential prayer, for they raise us up to God. And although in some cases we may not make our request explicitly, it is nonetheless hidden under the words, and even in the intention. Those who praise the divine greatness, those who thank Him for favors received, know (although they might not advert to it explicitly) that at His feet we are always

[22] Cf. Ps. 68:17 (RSV = Ps. 69:16): "Hear me, Lord, for Thy mercy is kind."

[23] Dan. 9:19.

souls in need, and that His goodness cannot fail to be moved at the sight of our indigence.

Often we collect together in one formula all the different kinds of prayer. In a word or two, we adore or thank, we ask for pardon and help, and approach the Father in the steps of the Son, in the arms of Mary, in union with all the company of Heaven. I cannot think of anything that could be dearer to the God of love or make a greater appeal to His love.

In the Gospels there are many forms of prayer ideal for all circumstances. The most beautiful, needless to say, is our Lady's "They have no wine."[24] The request itself is lost in the perfect act of trust. Mary is so sure of being heard. She feels that it would wound her Son's tenderness by asking directly for the wine. Jesus' love for her, His unfailing thoughtfulness for others, leave no doubt in her mind as to the answer. She speaks, and then waits, as all mothers do. And she invites us to do the same: "Whatsoever He shall say to you, do ye."[25]

And so do those two beloved of Jesus whom the Gospel calls Martha and Mary, at the bedside of Lazarus their brother. They know that Jesus loves them, and so they ask for nothing. They simply say, "Lord, he whom Thou lovest is sick."[26] There is no actual request, no word of their grief. They say, in effect, "You love . . . and someone is suffering." In that home, so united, the brother's sickness is their sickness, and they have not the slightest doubt that their common grief will find an echo in the heart of their Friend.

[24] John 2:3.
[25] John 2:5.
[26] Cf. John 11:3.

Chapter 7

Let prayer refresh your soul

Prayer should be continuous.[27] It is the soul breathing. Just as we have to breathe continuously, so we must pray continuously. Prayer is the deep interior movement of which we are barely conscious. To become aware of it, so far as we can, is indeed a great grace. To live, conscious of this movement and of Him who is both its source and term, is the greatest of all graces; indeed, it is Heaven on earth.

Onto this deep movement, the continuity of which is unhappily perceived by so few, should be grafted special prayers — that is, those that are more conscious and willed. It is these we properly call "prayers," and which call for fixed times. The times for these prayers in the case of priests and religious are so precise that they are called "Hours"; that is to say, certain prayers are attached to certain hours during the day and night. They are so determined that the whole day is, as it were, one continuous prayer. The repetition of these prayers turns our vacillating mind, so easily and so often distracted, back to God. Just when our mind could be caught up by some superficial thing, the time for the Divine Office comes around, and our mind is called away from the pressing vanities that might have occupied it and is plunged again in God.

[27] Cf. Luke 21:36: "Watch ye, therefore, praying at all times."

The Prayer of the Presence of God

The ordinary Christian is not held by so strict a tie. Regular hours for prayer, filling the day and canalizing everything toward God, is not for him a duty and a daily task. But what for him is not an obligation he may, of course, do out of love. I say out of love, but it is a love that is in his own interest. But even for him, there are fixed times when he ought to recollect himself and renew the divine contact. "In the morning," says the psalmist, "Thou shalt hear my voice. . . . In the morning I will stand before Thee."[28] And the prophet Isaiah: "In the morning early, I will watch to Thee,"[29] as if, for him, there could be no other awakening than this, and all time not so occupied was but night and sleep. Still more relevant is that other word of the son of Sirach, falling gently and spreading like dew: "[The wise man] will give his heart to resort early to the Lord that made him, and he will pray in the sight of the Most High."[30]

Sleep brings renewal; that is what the word *rest* or *repose* implies. It revives us, provided we put entirely out of our mind everything that has disturbed us during the day. If, on the other hand, we pursue in our dreams the things that have attracted us during our waking hours, our sleep only wearies us still further, instead of bringing us rest. Night is thus like a new creation: it relaxes the limbs, gives assurance to the mind, renews the soul, and restores our whole being. These hours of repose are hours of unconsciousness. We do not live this deep, restorative contact with our Source; the soul does not perceive Him. It wants this contact, and indeed achieves it, but it is not conscious of it. During these hours of sleep, it does not offer to God, who is still its all, the homage of

[28] Ps. 5:4-5 (RSV = Ps. 5:3).
[29] Isa. 26:9.
[30] Ecclus. 39:6 (RSV = Sir. 39:5).

the whole being for which it is responsible. There is a kind of break in the divine dialogue, for although the soul holds the first place in our being, it does not constitute, as we must recognize, our all.

When the body awakens in the morning, and the soul becomes again conscious of this "whole," it resumes command and becomes once more the link and interpreter of the created world, thus renewing its conscious contact with the Creator. That is why in the psalms at Lauds, we invite the whole of creation to take up again its interrupted praise: "All ye works of the Lord, bless the Lord; praise and exalt Him above all forever."[31] Thus sings the soul to all creation, which it salutes anew. These are images of Him whom the soul loves, and all creation responds as with one voice: "We are, because He is; we are, because He gives us being, and we are what He gives us to be."

During the night, these voices continue their praise, but the body, which is the link between the soul and creation and conveys these harmonies to the soul, is asleep. But once awake, those voices beat loudly but calmly at the gate of the body's senses; the soul hears them again, and the great hymn of praise — if man takes his place in it — is resumed.

Yet how many do take their place in this mighty hymn? How many are conscious of their role in it and execute it with love? How many, having rested and having awakened refreshed, put themselves once more in communion with this immense reservoir of energies that God offers them: physical energies of renewed light, so rich even in corporal resources; energies of the air refreshed and purified; energies of the vegetation that has renewed this air, carrying away all the unwholesome things accumulated by

[31] Dan. 3:57.

animal breathing; above all, spiritual energies. The very language of creation seems something new; everything comes to life, every-thing speaks, invites, pleads to make contact, to be admired and interpreted.

Between this renewed world and the rested man, a harmony, a perfect understanding is created, which becomes a fullness when united to the Source from whom it proceeds. It is prayer that achieves this union and completes the body's rest. It is the prelude to the day's movement and is its preparation. Mankind dies through not understanding this.

Thus plunged anew in God, who is in that creation to which He has given Himself, man can take up again his daily toil. In this He is not alone. He leans upon HIM WHO IS; he draws from Him both light and strength. Beyond what he does, he sees Him for whom and by whom he acts, and is united with Him in his task. His every act takes on an immense importance, outstrips the brief moment in which it is done, and is engraved in eternal duration.

A day is no longer just a day; it is a preparation and already a participation in eternity. Upon these heights, men can face the difficulties of this quickly passing life. He is not crushed by the testing time, nor frightened by temptation. When these things come, he renews, with one elevation of his soul, with one bound, as it were, toward God, his contact with the source of life and re-sists the temptation. To obtain such a consummation, prayer must really be prayer — that is, a raising of the mind and heart to God, a turning away from all created and human attractions.

Chapter 8

༄

Rejoice that God answers prayers

Answers to prayer: this is a difficult subject to write about, because it is so vast. And yet I must say something about it, because it reflects God's glory so much.

History is full of the answers to prayer. All the saints of the Old and New Testaments were great supplicants. Their lives were a continuous colloquy with God. He entered into everything, and they sought His assistance in all their needs. And God, they said repeatedly, always heard them. The movement of their souls toward Him, whether to ask for grace or to thank Him for it; whether to beg for the forgiveness of their sins or to praise the greatness of this best of Fathers, so real to them and so solicitous for their good — this is invariably the theme running through the Scriptures, or at least the predominant one.

The Psalms are full of the same idea. It runs through them like an incredibly rich and abundant sap, the sap of true life, simple yet strong, and expressive of all that is deepest in us. It is a theme we can repeat endlessly, and like all love's expressions, it never tires. It would seem to possess eternal youth and freshness and, ever new, grows with repetition ever greater and more splendid.

At times, it seems to us as though God departs from the order He has established, when He hears the voices of His friends begging him to do so. This order is beautiful indeed. The divine perfections are reflected in lines we can barely discern, but which we are never tired of admiring.

Dearly would I love to follow up this thought, but I would not know where to stop! Let the following suffice:

Springs gush forth from rocks in the desert;[32] the waters of the sea of rivers divide to allow a vast concourse of people to pass over.[33] The walls of cities fall down,[34] enemies are put to flight,[35] and manna descends daily from Heaven.[36] The sick are healed, the lame walk,[37] and the dead are raised to life.[38] Hardened sinners are touched by grace, while the minds of men are elevated so that they perceive beyond them perspectives of light by which they almost seem to enter into the very truth of God. Wills are strengthened and at once take control of passions until then unleashed. Divine Love comes so near to souls that He seems almost to consume them and to transform them into His own likeness.[39]

Such and even more wonderful things, which can be revealed to my dazed sight only by the light from beyond — this is what prayer can do. This is what it has done and is continually doing. In face of all this, I can only remain silent. When discussing these things it is easy enough to find words and phrases in which to express the movement of the mind when concerned with the things of God. But when it is a question of making known God's action to

---

[32] Num. 20:11.
[33] Exod. 14:21; Heb. 11:29; Josh. 3:16.
[34] Josh. 6:20; Heb. 11:30.
[35] Cf. Lev. 26:8.
[36] Exod. 16:15.
[37] Matt. 8:16.
[38] Luke 8:54-55.
[39] Cf. Deut. 4:24.

the world, above all to the world of souls, mere human language is altogether inadequate to describe the reality. We must either give up the attempt or return to the unfailing simplicity of what the Holy Spirit tells us in the sacred Scriptures.

Chapter 9

Ask for God alone

When praying to God, we can only ask for God, since He is everything, and in giving Himself, He gives us all. In asking for Him, we
ask for all. When we possess Him, we can wish and ask for nothing
more. Once we grasp this truth, there is no point in writing or saying anything; we are content simply to pray, and even then we
would ask for nothing. The whole of the first part of the Our Father keeps us on these silent heights. That is all we see there, for
God is both the source and the object of our asking. "Hallowed be
Thy name, Thy kingdom come, Thy will be done. . . ."[40] What
more can we ask?

We could even do without the words, content with the interior
movement of the soul, which says all in silence. Or we can think of
the words and develop them. This is what so many profitable
prayers do in fact, both in public and in private, according to the
temperaments of different people. Insofar as they remain on this
essential level of God's glory, the coming of His kingdom and the
fulfillment of His will, they are good. The actual words or thoughts
with which we clothe them matters little. When a person loves,
he is conscious only of love. Now, God is our Father; that is to say,
He is all love. Holy Scripture never tires of telling us that He

[40] Matt. 6:9-10.

knows perfectly well what is good for us. We cannot do better, therefore, than to leave all to Him.

We may nevertheless make known our needs and express our wishes to Him, on this indispensable condition of our submission to His loving will. This is what our Lord would have us learn from the second part of the Our Father. This is what the innumerable and beautiful prayers of the Church, of the Mass, and of the Divine Office teach us. For they all come from the Holy Spirit, who has inspired them.

The first question to be considered is what order we should follow in our prayers. This has been decided in principle long ago. The order to follow is God's order. We must ask for all that may contribute (and in the measure in which it will contribute) to His glory, and the advancement of His kingdom. That is why the first and essential object, and the one we must never lose sight of, is our eternal salvation and our union with God. This is the end of all prayer and of every movement of the soul: to praise God, to be united with Him, to be transformed into His likeness forever; to become forever His image and His child.

This end necessitates certain means that lead to it. We cannot ask for our salvation without asking for virtues and grace. Grace is divine life in the soul; the virtues are the means through which grace is effective. Grace is given to us in the form of a seed, and we are, as it were, newborn children. In us, as in a child just born, is the seed of all subsequent development of life, and this seed is given to us in Baptism. As yet the developments have not taken place, but they are there, just as the stem, the branches, the leaves, and the blossoms are in the seed cast into the ground. We cannot, therefore, reasonably ask for union with God without asking also for these developments, which will go toward the making of the desired union. To do otherwise would be to prevent ourselves from growing in Him,[41] or to want grace to remain an undeveloped seed in the depths of our soul.

So far, all is clear, and the object of our prayer is obvious. But there are certain things that might or might not serve to bring us closer to God; we do not know. It is the same with what we call natural evil. I have gold in my keeping. I can use it for the glory of God and the good of my soul, or the precise opposite. An illness can help to sanctify me, provided I bear it with patience and for the love of our heavenly Father, since He permits it. Or I can accept it, but in a spirit of rebellion and hating God for sending it.

In view of all this, what attitude must I adopt when I pray? I must wait quietly in a spirit of confiding trust, without wasting any time in reasoning on vain suppositions, but rest in the great reality. That great reality is this: God is good, and He is love. He wants only my happiness, and I entrust to Him the care of obtaining it for me. It is the same even with supernatural values. A very young child — what does he do? He nestles against his father's heart, happy in his love. He just stays there, content to wait. This quiet expectancy is not a passive indifference; it is an unwavering trust, which is the form desire takes. Only the desire must be there always, and it must be the real source of the repose; otherwise this repose would be mere idleness.

As a rule, the Holy Spirit, who inspires our prayers, tells us to make them more explicit. There are advantages in this. The thought of the supernatural happiness awaiting us, of how enviable it is, stimulates the desire, which must always be ardent yet always remaining calm. All the saints possessed ardent desires.

---

[41] Cf. Eph. 4:15: "But, doing the truth in charity, we may in all things grow up in Him who is the head, even Christ."

The Prayer of the Presence of God

Ardor, however, is not the same as violence. What we should keep before our minds is the wonderful power of grace and virtue; of what grace is accomplishing in our souls; of the eternal salvation that is our goal; of the glory it will give to God and the boundless happiness in store for us. To contemplate long these truths is one of the highest forms of prayer that we can have in this life, and it will pass one day easily into the vision of God in the life to come.

Chapter 10

Assist your prayer with various means

There are certain exterior aids that help the soul to rise above itself and above things, in its ascent toward the sacred heights. Our physical posture is one that can be of considerable assistance. The reason for this is the close link between the soul and the body.

We are all familiar with the joined hands, the outstretched arms, and the eyes raised to Heaven. Moses, during the fierce battle between his people and the Amaleckites, remained with his hands outstretched. As he grew weary, Aaron and Hur supported them so that we would not abandon this gesture of supplication.[42] When our Lord came to the tomb where lay the body of Lazarus, intending to raise him up to life, He lifted His eyes to Heaven but remained standing.[43] During his agony he knelt and then prostrated himself."[44] He came as close as possible to that earth to which He had descended, in order to raise it up with Him above its nature, and to take it with Him to His Father. All these different variants show us how necessary it is to be always ready to adopt the attitude the Holy Spirit suggests to us, and not feel constrained to assume any particular posture unless it is clearly indicated.

[42] Exod. 17:11-12.
[43] John 11:12.
[44] Mark 14:35; Luke 22:41.

The Prayer of the Presence of God

There are other aids that are interior and more spiritual. They are of two kinds, or rather, they come from two sources. One source is within us. The sight of our misery gives birth in us to the desire to be delivered from it, and to call upon Him from whom alone can come this aid. If the thought of our helplessness, which is continually asserting itself by repeated falls, becomes permanent, prayer becomes little by little the habitual movement of the soul, and gradually we approach the idea proposed by our Lord, when He said we "ought always to pray, and not to faint."[45] Thus we lift ourselves above the short moment of this fleeting life, and enter God's eternal duration. The thought of ourselves causes us to go out of ourselves and lose ourselves in God.

Other motives we find outside ourselves. The most important is the need to glorify God. Indeed, we can say not only that it is the principal source, but that it is the only source, for all others come back to it. Such is the thought of the divine Master, who came to teach us how to pray; who gave us the perfect model and whose whole life was a prayer — a prayer, however, that was not a raising of the mind and heart, since He never left the summit where God dwells. It is equally profitable to have recourse to those who have closely imitated this perfect model, such as St. John the solitary of Patmos,[46] or St. Mary Magdalen in her wild grotto. To think of such as these strongly encourages us to follow their example. In asking their aid, we feel certain that it will be given at once, and that their hands uplifted to God on our behalf are also outstretched toward us to support and raise us up. Indeed, the whole of the heavenly court is ready to assist the faltering steps of God's children.

---

[45] Luke 18:1.

[46] That is, St. John the Evangelist, who was exiled on the island of Patmos.

Chapter 11

⌒

Practice almsgiving and humility

Much has been written about the "wings of prayer," and very fine
things, too. At first sight, their diversity places us rather at a disad-
vantage. Writers speak of two wings, because that would seem to
be required by the comparison. But they differ widely when it
comes to describing them. For St. John Chrysostom[47] it is almsgiving and fasting; for Hugh of St. Victor[48] it is the thought of our
weakness and of the divine mercy. For others it is compunction and
tears; for others again, trust and obedience, justice and humility.
All of them are right; these are all divine energies that come to our
aid and lead us to God.

Almsgiving, the giving of what we possess and of our love for
these possessions to such as are in need, is a divine resemblance,
which gives us a strong claim on divine Love Himself, whose
greatest desire is precisely union in resemblance. God gives to
those who give, and in the measure in which they give. This is
what our Lord so often emphasized in short and striking phrases:

---

[47] St. John Chrysostom (c. 347-407), Archbishop of Con-
stantinople and Doctor; named Chrysostom, or "Golden
Mouth" for his eloquent preaching.

[48] Hugh of St. Victor (1096-1141), philosopher, theologian, and mystical writer.

The Prayer of the Presence of God

"Give, and it shall be given to you."[49] Every act of kindness is yet another feather in the wings of prayer, which makes them all the stronger.

Fasting is an alms given directly to God. It is for His sake that we fast. It is in order that we may become more strongly attached to Him that we deprive ourselves of that food which comes from Him, and of which we can partake only for His sake. To offer Him the sacrifice of what is not absolutely indispensable for our physical well being is thus to raise ourselves from our level to His. This is itself a prayer: it raises us up to His level, to His presence, and is the prelude to many intimate colloquies of the highest form of prayer.

The thought of our own misery, and of the unfathomable divine mercy, also lifts us up to the same heights. They are, as it were, two oceans spreading beyond the narrowness of our individual selves and meeting in the infinite. For we can see our nothingness only in the light of the divine greatness. Otherwise we see only a very superficial part of it, and this is more than we can bear. In the light of this immense love, which stoops down to it in order to raise it up and enfold it with His greatness, our misery becomes the greatest of all realities. That reality opens to the soul the horizons of love, where He who is truth and love awaits us and says to the soul, "Come and stay here forever."

The source of all true prayers is there. To admit our misery is to be truly humble, with that humility which has its roots in love and is nourished and perfected by it — that humility which says, "I am nothing; God is all. Yet He offers Himself to me, and in Him I possess all things." The act of believing in God's mercy is an act of justice (which is rendering to others what is due to them). That act of

49 Luke 6:38.

42

faith is *due* to God. He loves to give Himself to our nothingness, even if that nothingness has offended Him.

And so, all these ideas meet in one point. One or another is put forward by various writers, according to the insights given them by the Holy Spirit. For it is He who directs their secret thoughts.[50] Thus, all souls, whose diversity is known to the same Spirit, come there to drink the water they need.

[50] Cf. John 3:8: "The Spirit breatheth where He will."

Part 2

Perfecting Your Prayer

Chapter 12

≈

Detach yourself from earthly things

The soul that prays raises itself to God, stands in His presence, and speaks to Him — a raising up and holy converse; otherwise it is not prayer.

Arrived at these heights, the soul speaks. The very movement that accomplishes this is already a kind of speech; it is the answer to God's love and is, as it were, the whisperings of that love in us. The Spirit, Love Himself, inspires, raises, and bears upward the soul, drawn by these heights.

There follows a weaning from all earthly things, which is simplicity. The soul is henceforth indifferent to everything except this one infinitely pure object. It leaves everything, is indifferent to everything, for the sake of this object. It wills to be united with Him, to enter into intimate relations with Him that will be unfettered, to be alone with Him alone.

The soul is purified by this detachment. Here is a thought of inexhaustible depth.

The soul is a mirror — a living mirror, which gives itself to things and is united to them, causing them to enter into itself. Inferior to the soul, these external objects drag it down and spoil its purity, like a speck of dust on a spotless garment.

The soul is made for God. He alone is great enough and noble enough for it. Everything else strains and belittles it and drags it down to a lower level. The soul is no longer in God's presence, and any kind of intimate relationship is impossible. If the soul speaks to God, it is from afar, like people who do not as yet know one another and remain at a distance.

☞

Chapter 13

Unite your will with God's

There is a very simple way to attain to this divine height. It is perfect submission to all that God wills. Distances disappear, and true union results. When the soul wishes only what the loved one wills, there is perfect union, and prayer becomes the soul's very life. Everything becomes prayer, and the soul prays always. This is probably the meaning of our Lord's counsel that we ought always to pray. It is certainly the simplest and surest way to do so.

This union of wills makes for conformity: the human will becomes identified with the divine will. It is always one with God's will, and therefore always as pure as God Himself. In the midst of complications it remains simple, for we no longer want either the many things in which we are involved or the works we do, but simply Him who wills the things and asks these acts of us.

Unity, purity, simplicity: if we probe beneath the surface of the multiplicity of these expressions, we always find again the unique reality that expresses itself in these different ways, and which, through them, leads us to HIM WHO IS. And that reality is Love's Breath, who comes from Him and returns to Him. It is the Spirit of love praying in the soul who, in order that it may pray, makes the soul submissive, pure, simple, adoring, and loving; and makes it pray in order that it may become so more and more.

Chapter 14

⌒

Revere God

Love and fear are not opposed to one another. Fear is born of love and protects and develops it. When we love, we fear: we fear to lose the one we love; we fear to displease him, to see him go away; we fear to see his love grow less.

Fear is the measure of love, which, in turn, is proportioned to fear. Fear and love act in consort and produce the balanced harmony of our relations with the August Majesty, who is infinite compassion. Before the greatness that offers itself we feel small and unworthy. We forget the wonder of the perfection that would overwhelm us with dismay, before the compassionate goodness that invites us to take refuge in its outstretched arms. The one safeguards us from carelessness and want of respect; the other draws us and gives us confidence. And our prayer finds, without any effort, under the guidance of the Holy Spirit, the happy balance between dismay and presumption.

A want of reverence in prayer is by no means rare. It paralyzes the majority of souls. It is what wounds God's relations with His children; the idea of a Father is spoiled. He is a companion, a friend, a confidant whom we treat as an equal. A father is altogether different. He is someone from whom we receive everything; to whom we give only what he gives to us. In his presence a child remains, and must remain, one who comes from him, and can act only by his power. The father is the source, the author, without whom the child is nothing and can do nothing. The child depends on him for everything and in everything, and lives in a state of complete and constant submission to him. Love changes nothing of this: it tempers the submission with a confiding love, but it does not do away with it or diminish it in any way.

How the angels and truly devout souls realize this! For them, God remains God. They surround His throne, and an invincible power binds them to Him, draws them, and holds them, forcing them to lose themselves in the abyss of His love, which is His very being. It evokes from them hymns of praise, of ardent adoration. But that same power makes them prostrate themselves before him, veiling their faces.[51] It causes a tremor to pass through their whole being, which is never one of dismay but remains always one of deep respect.

Yet for His earthly children God is a judge, a Father whom we have aggrieved. The soul that prays can never forget this. The divine face is truth and life. The soul has turned away from it, preferring untruth and death. And God has received the soul back and has effaced its sins; but the tendencies and the potentialities remain, reminding the soul of what it has done and can do again.

These sins have left their mark on the face of the Man of Sorrows — deep marks caused by suffering, the price of the soul's sins, recalling Love's pursuit in the steps of the soul's wanderings. For love of the soul, Love had to become Mercy — a love ever bent toward the soul's misery, in order to lift it up. And the soul has evaded the embrace of the open arms. Under whatever form the soul pictures divine Love, God always remains the most misunderstood and the most repulsed of beings.

[51] Cf. Isa. 6:2.

So when we pray, we must stand in His presence, on His level. We must see His suffering in the same way that we see His greatness, and as we picture His compassion. But we must also remember that that suffering, that greatness and that compassion will one day judge us. We shall be weighed in the balance by them; and if we are found wanting in any way, we shall hear the words: "Depart from me. . . ."[52] "Go elsewhere; go to those who refused to be my friends."

[52] Matt. 25:41.

Chapter 15

⌒

Pray with attention

These thoughts, born of love, draw us toward Him to whom they are directed, and this we call *attention*. An attentive soul is a soul powerfully drawn toward the object that attracts it. A careless soul is one that allows itself to be drawn by other objects. Attention depends upon the importance we attach to the object that beckons us, and on the degree of attraction it exercises. If we know it as something important and beautiful, as something good and powerful; if we know that it is without flaw and rich enough to satisfy all our desires, then our attention becomes very great.

Attention to God is rare, because very few really know Him. Sin has drawn us away from Him. We live surrounded by created things; their images fill our minds; they grip us and make attention to God difficult. We have to turn round again; that is what the word *conversion* means.

There are many degrees in conversion. Only the saints are truly converted; they alone have "turned around" completely. This complete turning around means that henceforth we want only to attend to God. Gradually, with the help of grace and after many attempts more or less prolonged, we fix our attention on Him.

The daily — and often more than daily — repetition of the same acts and of the same formulas is a danger. Habit can easily become routine. Prayer becomes a mechanical process, without reference to the mind or heart. Only our lips speak to God. But He is a Spirit and wants to communicate to us His spiritual life. While our lips move thoughtlessly, we are carried away by our imagination in a thousand directions, and it is with all sorts of things and persons — above all with ourselves — that we hold converse. Our attention wanders because love is wanting; and prayer, which should set us on fire, merely deepens the rift between God and ourselves, which our negligence has gradually created. Coldness begets inattention, itself begotten of ignorance, and so we slip — more rapidly than we think — down the slopes of lukewarmness, at the end of which may be death.

What is important, however, much more than inattention of the mind is inattention of the will. The former is often beyond our control. There are inattentive prayers that delight the heart of our Lord. When we make an effort to place and keep ourselves in His presence, and certain dispositions of body and soul repeatedly prevent us, in spite of ourselves, from perceiving and retaining that beloved presence; when our desire for the Beloved suffers tortures from our powerlessness; when we humbly accept that distress, the distraction becomes an exceptionally precious and powerful means to union. For, in our relations with God, all is measured by love; and any feeling of repugnance for created objects in order to be united with the uncreated God is love.

Attention to the words we pronounce and to our actions is good, and is almost always sufficient, and often to be preferred; sometimes it is all we can manage. The important thing is to realize the definition of prayer: the soul, freed from what is transitory, turns and tends to our heavenly Father, by whatsoever ways and means it can. As soon as contact is made, the soul prays; when that contact is fervent, the prayer is excellent.

Chapter 16

⌒

Guard your heart

Creatures — and the Devil, who uses them — do not let themselves be ousted without a struggle. The life of prayer calls for continuous battles. It is the most important and the longest effort in a life dedicated to God. This effort has been given a beautiful name: it is called *the guard of the heart*.

The human heart is a city; it was meant to be a stronghold. Sin surrendered it. Henceforth it is an open city, the walls of which have to be built up again.[53] The enemy never ceases to do all he can to prevent this. He does this with his accustomed cleverness and strength, with stratagem and fury. He puts before us such happy thoughts (and occasionally useful ones), pictures so attractive or frightening, and he clothes it all with reasons so impressive that he succeeds all along the line to distract us and entice us away from the divine presence.

We must always be starting again. These continual recoveries, this endless beginning again, tires and disheartens us far more than the actual fighting. We would much prefer a real battle, fierce and decisive. But God, as a rule, thinks otherwise. He would rather we were in a constant state of war. He prefers these ambuscades and snares; these precautions and the need for constant vigilance. He

---

[53] Ps. 50:20 (RSV = Ps. 51:18).

is love, and this continuous warfare[54] calls for more love and develops that love still further. Besides, He is there: He conducts the fight Himself. He holds the enemy in check, watches his every movement, and outmaneuvers him. He plays with him, allows him to advance in order the better to attack and overcome him. He prefers striking victories, in spite of temporary setbacks, and sometimes even real disasters.

We must detach ourselves from this world. The simple, mechanical repetition of words is not enough. Distractions voluntarily entertained paralyze it; occupations become preoccupations and are an obstacle. We do not give God His due. We give Him nothing unless we give Him all the attention of which we are capable. To what tasks, what cares, what useless preoccupations do we not attach undue importance, and what a place they take up in our prayers. We think we are seeking only the kingdom of God and His glory, and all the while we are seeking ourselves. Such things are not inspired by the Holy Spirit, but by nature. The Devil is at hand to tell us how extremely profitable they are. Indeed, he encourages and helps us, and actually makes them with us, for they weaken the divine union and the heart's sweet contact.

For a heart that is calm and free, that keeps itself detached and turned toward God, all occupation is prayer. For the heart that gives itself up completely to its tasks and thus forgets God, even prayer is sterile and a waste of time.

---

[54] Cf. Job 7:1: "The life of man upon earth is a warfare."

Chapter 17

☙

Place yourself in God's presence

True prayer is perhaps very rare, because of the lack of this necessary basis: the placing of ourselves in the presence of the divine Person whom we are addressing. We do not know, we do not think, we do not sufficiently realize that He is there with us, looking at us, listening, speaking, loving, and giving Himself. Too often He is only someone present to our mind, soon replaced by others. He is not "the soul's sweet Guest," our friend and Father. Before beginning to pray, we should remind ourselves of this emphatically again and again; we should make it live, just as we make other things live by becoming absorbed in them.

Our act of faith at that moment must be an act of the soul, and not merely a mental act, which says, "This is so." The soul says nothing; it opens out to welcome and surrender itself to the light. It allows itself to be taken and invaded; it becomes what it receives. Then God is present to it, just as it is present to itself, although in a different manner. Then prayer becomes a living reality. The Holy Spirit, the life-giving Spirit, prays in us, uttering the inexpressible cry: "Abba, Father."[55]

And He makes us understand what this means. He reveals the divine communication of life in progress at that moment in the

---

[55] Gal. 4:6.

soul through Him. He reveals it "in the face of Christ Jesus."⁵⁶ The soul sees Jesus; it sees His veritable and glorious countenance, "the glory of the only-begotten of the Father."⁵⁷ He reveals Jesus: "He shall glorify me."⁵⁸ He reveals Him in a clear and blinding light, and the soul sees in Him the Father giving Himself. The Son does what the Father does.⁵⁹ If He gives Himself unreservedly, it is because He sees the Father giving Himself unreservedly. It is thus that the Spirit, proceeding from them both, places them before one another, illuminating one another, unceasingly pouring themselves into one another, and, without confusion of substance — indeed maintaining and manifesting their distinction — makes them "perfected in one."⁶⁰ Then prayer is true prayer.

---

⁵⁶ 2 Cor. 4:6.
⁵⁷ John 1:14.
⁵⁸ John 16:14.
⁵⁹ Cf. John 14:31.
⁶⁰ Cf. John 17:23.

⌒

Chapter 18

Persevere in prayer

Man is subject to a severe trial, which comes from his very nature. He has all the potentialities of a spirit, but has to realize them in a body. While the spirit is quick, matter is cumbersome. The spirit perceives in a flash, and at once desires what it sees. By this dual act, it achieves its end and rests in it. Matter only slowly receives what acts on it. These external actions have to be passed on from molecule to molecule, from cell to cell, from the muscles to the nerves, from them to the nerve centers and thence by one's sensitivity, a channel neither wholly material nor wholly spiritual, and thus by the intermediary of the internal senses, rejoin the spiritual parts of our being, where they become ideas. These ideas, in turn, are by the same channels passed on to the executive organs. It needs any number of such impressions coming from without to constitute ourselves, and it needs as many again for our personality to realize itself *in act*.

Now, our relations with God follow the same law. As a rule, our understanding of faith comes from outside us and progresses according to the movement of our nature. The Holy Spirit may intervene personally, following higher laws, and often does. Then the approach to God assumes an easier and quicker pace, altogether special and delightful. But this is not the normal way, and we cannot count on it. Usually, we follow our own slow pace, which the Holy Spirit directs and aids, but without suppressing or modifying it.

We must go, therefore, to God by the supernatural, which takes control of human knowledge and the natural virtues, and follow (if we would find Him) the way that leads to the development of our nature. During the course of this development, we are more or less sustained in the natural order by the need to find a place in the sun, and to provide for our wants; by the desire for success and tangible results. But even with these incentives, few become really zealous, while those who are disheartened are all too numerous. For the most part, we do just what is necessary (when we do anything at all!). In the spiritual order, the quest for God is not maintained, at least not to the same extent, by such tangible results.

To the wayfarer on earth, God never refuses to give Himself, but He does often hide Himself. He likes us to seek Him and go on seeking Him, to have confidence in Him. He would have us ask without receiving; to renew again and again our efforts that seem fruitless. In other words, it is perseverance in prayer that He loves.[61]

---

[61] Cf. Matt. 10:22: "He that shall persevere unto the end, he shall be saved."

Chapter 19

Have confidence in God

Perseverance is the fruit of confidence, while confidence in our relations with God is the surest form of love. It is born of faith. It presupposes a right idea of God. The confident soul has had to develop in itself a knowledge of those divine perfections which are in fact the same as the divine Being and infinite Love, but which, as we see them, are, as it were, rays tempered by the prism of creatures. How we need to read and to meditate before these perfections can become present in us — living, powerful ideas — and so come to the surface when the way is dark and we need them to light up a road that is at all times difficult.

Only those who love, who are full of and sustained by the Spirit of love, have the courage to undertake and pursue a study that must be constantly renewed. Everything depends upon that. This study is the fertilizing spring that flows in the soul, causing the desert to blossom with spring flowers and autumn fruits.[62] Our Lord repeatedly says in the Gospel, "Have confidence";[63] and He says the same thing again and again to the soul that loves: "He that shall persevere to the end, he shall be saved."[64]

[62] Cf. Isa. 35:1.
[63] Cf. Matt. 9:22.
[64] Matt. 24:13.

The Prayer of the Presence of God

Confidence is not presumption. The confident soul does not forget that prayer is a relationship, and that, although one of the terms is infinitely powerful and good, the other is extremely weak and to be pitied. The knowledge of these two terms creates in the soul a just sense of the very subtle disposition that must govern these divine relations. The soul constantly hears our Lord's reiterated recommendation: *We ought always to pray,* and His other word: *Watch.*[65]

Confidence in God in general and in particular is a disposition of the soul of which it is difficult to speak, because it is difficult to explain exactly what it is. There is nothing to compare it with, no landmarks, as it were, in the order of nature. It depends on certain perfections of which the world offers us no equivalent. There are men who are really good and full of kindness and charity; who have a genuine affection for us and are always ready to do us a kindness. They will do their utmost to help. But their "utmost" is restricted, extremely so; and even their dispositions can change. "And which of you, if he ask of his father bread, will he give him a stone?"[66] In a father, the paternal instinct is always uncertain; with men, evil is always possible. In God, there is only good; He can will and do only what is good for us. And if we ask Him for the Spirit of His Son, who is the supreme good, how surely and abundantly will He grant our request. The proof has been given us: "He gave his only-begotten Son."[67] After that, even the thought of a refusal to our prayer is impossible. "Ask, and it shall be given you; seek, and you shall find; knock, and it shall be opened to you."[68]

[65] Matt. 26:41.
[66] Luke 11:11.
[67] John 3:16.
[68] Luke 11:9.

Chapter 20

☞

Understand why God makes you wait

Why does God, who is love, keep us waiting? Because He is love, and seeks love. Love that does not know how to wait is not love. To love is to give ourselves. Not only for a fraction of a lifetime, nor with a part of its strength: love is, and seeks, the total gift of self.

Love is based on esteem. We love only what we value and admire. We love only the "good." What is too easily and too quickly come by does not attract deep souls. It becomes a superficial good, which cannot satisfy the rich capacity of their nature. And they are right. The relations between beings are governed by laws, which they guess at but cannot always define. It is a law that real treasures are deeply buried and carefully hidden; that serious acquisitions call for proportionate efforts. What exceptions there are do not weaken the argument.

God is *the* treasure beyond price. Were He to give Himself too easily, even the best would turn their backs upon Him. St. John Climacus[69] gives a similar reason, but with an interesting difference. "Prayer," he says, "is an activity that develops and enriches

---

[69] St. John Climacus (d. c. 649), abbot of the monastery of Mount Sinai and author of the mystical work *Ladder to Paradise*.

enormously. It is a source of merit and satisfaction, and of spiritual progress of every kind." God imposes repetitions and a certain persistence in prayer in order to increase our merit. Delays in union are not time lost; far from it. God sees very far ahead; He makes wonderful use of what we call evil — of our wanderings, our hesitations and detours, although He does not love them or want them. It is at these moments, above all, that we need confidence and perseverance. The prayer, whether for ourselves or for others, that is not discouraged, which persists and besieges Heaven, touches God's heart; and that is why He tells us to persevere.

Chapter 21

☙

Pray with persistence

God is love.[70] He loves and wants to be loved; it is the basic law of
His being. To realize this is to find the solution to all our problems.
A soul that tends toward Him cannot tire Him. It always delights Him, and the soul should know this. Its persistence displeases Him only when it is for something it wants inordinately.
For example, I want good health, and I insist. Such a request could
displease Him, because I must want — at all costs, that is — only
what He wills; and health is not in His eyes essential. He is sad-
dened, not by my persistence, but because an irregular wish such as
this separates me from Him.

When it is a question of the real good, of such things as He always wills and for which we can ask Him without being separated
from Him, our persistence pleases Him. It is what our Lord Himself commended in a few delightful parables: the child asking his
father for bread;[71] the friend knocking repeatedly at his friend's door
for the same reason;[72] and the widow who persevered in asking a
judge (a wicked one at that) for justice, until she obtained it.[73]

[70] 1 John 4:16.
[71] Matt. 7:9.
[72] Luke 11:5-8.
[73] Luke 18:2-6.

The Prayer of the Presence of God

God is a Father, a friend, and a judge. But he is a Father whose love is boundless, and whose power is as great as His love. He is a friend whose friendship knows no change, and is at the mercy of all our needs. He is a judge, but always just, always moved by our appeals and quick to answer them. He loves our persistence; He wants us to appeal to Him, to ask of Him, so that He can be sure of our love, and taste the joy of having a proof of it, even if it be a selfish one.

Chapter 22

⌒

Avoid lengthy prayers

It is not the length of our prayers that gives them value, but their fervor or love. If love needs much time in which to express itself, by all means let it persist in its ardor and in the movement by which it expresses itself. If, on the other hand, a word or even a thought raises the soul to God; if it remains there silent and rapt; if, called to other duties, it impregnates its outward activities with its inward atmosphere in which the divine Bridegroom gives Himself with His "touches" — all this is unquestionably good.

What about prescribed prayers? We must faithfully fulfill our obligations. What about prayers of our own choice? Here we must follow the divine movement that inspires and directs them. When that movement passes, we must cease. The soul may carry on for a little while, so as to make quite sure that the interior inspiration has ceased, and to show that it does not stop of its own accord. After that, it can carry on with what it has to do, or rest, as the case may be; but it must always remain at the disposal of the Master and attentive to Him.[74]

Lengthy prayers can be dangerous. They tire us and open the door to distractions, which, even though they may be involuntary, should be avoided as far as possible; they can lead to routine. A

---

[74] Cf. John 11:28: "The Master is come and calleth for thee."

rapid movement carrying the soul upward and often renewed, thus assuring the continuity of our ardor, is much better. That was the method used by the Fathers of the desert. It had to be abandoned for active work. Now, before entering on their duties, the monks who are vowed to work make a good foundation of union first thing in the morning, by staying an hour or so with their Beloved. They set aside this time expressly for Him, because they know they cannot count on coming back to Him as they would like. It is a necessity. They are then able to master, as far as they can, the unreliability of human attention, and thus lay in a store of energies for the whole day. But the ancient method is still of value for contemplative souls.

But these considerations are beside the point; they touch only on the fringe of prayer. The length of our personal prayers of devotion depend upon Him who prays in us. They must be what He wants them to be. Now, He wants to raise up the soul and keep it in His presence as long as possible. The soul that has put aside obstacles and keeps itself free so that God may take possession of it is a soul that prays. It has been caught up in an upward movement — a movement in God and toward God. To prolong it or to discontinue it is good; to resume and continue it is also good. All that is regulated by the divine movement is good.

The Fathers of the desert prayed by short upliftings of the heart. They also prayed by long outpourings of their soul plunged in God. St. Anthony[75] passed nights in this state and reproached the sun for depriving him of his beloved light. Another father remained for fourteen consecutive days standing motionless with his hands uplifted and his arms outstretched. "What do we do now?"

[75] St. Anthony of Egypt (251-356), desert monk and father of Western monasticism.

Avoid lengthy prayers

Abbot Loth asked an old anchorite named Joseph. Joseph stood up, stretched out his arms, raised his hands, and his fingers became like burning lamps. "That is what you can do," he said, "if you want to; your whole being can be transfigured into fire."

Long prayers or short prayers, provided they are influenced and transformed by the Spirit of love, all are *according to God*.[76] If we let ourselves be overcome by distractions or drowsiness, then they can lose much of their value.

[76] Cf. 1 John 5:14: "This is the confidence which we have toward Him: that whatsoever we shall ask according to His will, He heareth us."

Chapter 23

Ponder God's greatness

The greatness of God, the nothingness of man: all religion is governed by this double reality, of which it makes a single whole, knit together and ruled by love. God *is*; man *is not*. God and being are one thing: man *is* only if God communicates being to him. Religion is born of that communication, and prayer, which is only religion in act, is the movement of the soul recognizing that it is receiving something and that it has only what it receives. To acknowledge this is essentially prayer, and it is humility.

That is why the Our Father is the perfect prayer, and the perfect summary of the religious life. The Father is undoubtedly He who gives all, but He is also HE WHO IS. He gives only because He is, and He gives what He is. All the splendors of creation are gathered up in this word *love*, and we should see them there when we pronounce it. With a rapid glance, we should picture to ourselves these innumerable created beings of whom we know so little: beings that enchant and dazzle us, and represent so much wisdom and power.

We should adore these perfections in Him who, in the depths of our being, gives Himself, forms us, and communicates to us all that we have of being and of life. Then we should remain in His presence, prostrate at His feet, conscious only of our nothingness. This is humility.

The Prayer of the Presence of God

God wants this attitude and cannot but want it. It is the point of departure of all He does in us, the foundation of the edifice He wants to build. He looks for that attitude and brings it about; and He must do this before He can commence His work; it is this which turns us toward Him. Hitherto we have been turned toward ourselves. Humility is implicit in faith, in the respectful and adoring submission of the soul at prayer.

I am afraid I am going to repeat myself. Formerly I should not have dared to do so; I would have thought it was to speak to no purpose. Now I find immense advantages and sweetness in doing so.

We speak expressly of what we love and to the One we love. I love, then, to repeat that God is great; that He is Lord as well as Father; that all excellence is in Him; that all the perfections gathered together and prolonged infinitely cannot express the unique and full richness of His being. Even a life spent in contemplating this mystery and in meditating on it, in going deeper into it, in seeing in the work of God images that can give us some idea of it, leaves us far, very far, infinitely far, from the reality. This reality is always beyond, very far beyond, all we can express or conceive.

That is why we must be humble. Before this immensity, overflowing all times, all beings, all their characteristics and perfections, the tiny minute I have to live, the small space I fill, the limits of my being and of my activity that I touch at every moment; the knowledge of my weakness, of my nothingness — all this is revealed and made obvious. It puts me in my place, and makes me feel quite tiny in that nothingness, to which God gives existence. If to that I add the thought of my sins; if I see this "nothingness" opposed to HIM WHO IS, daring to rebel against Him or, what is perhaps worse, become indifferent to Him, treating Him as if He were not, then I feel myself in an abyss.

Chapter 24

⌒

Understand the power of humility

But that very abyss is my salvation, if I only knew. "He that shall humble himself shall be exalted," says Incarnate Truth.[77] "God," says St. James, "resisteth the proud, and giveth grace to the humble."[78] I understand that, and I understand that Truth should speak thus, and that the Almighty should act in this way. Truth is an exact relationship between two terms that are being compared. The relationship between God and man is that God is Being Himself and man nothingness. When I recognize this, I am in harmony with God, who is Truth; we are in right relations. I am in a state of mind that He loves, and He has pity on me.

God desires nothing so much as to have pity on us and to come to our aid. He wants — I might almost say "impatiently," were He capable of impatience — to be allowed to help. For the name of *Being* that I give Him is incomplete. This BEING WHO IS is essential love, the gift of self. To give Himself is His life; He does nothing else.

Eternally the Father gives to the Son that infinite being of which He is the source, the ocean, the principle, and the term. Eternally, the Son, animated by this movement that this Father

[77] Matt. 23:12.
[78] James 4:6.

communicates to Him, does the same thing toward His Father —
or better, in his Father. He gives back this gift by which they are
united and bound to one another, held the one in the other. Like
an ardent fire, which would be at the same time a mirror, the Father is reproduced in the Son, who reproduces the Father. The
Love who unites them proceeds from them both and, in His turn,
reproduces them, illumines them, and manifests them. Thence He
passes to overflow and communicate Himself to beings who, animated by the same movement, will give themselves as They give
Themselves, being united to Them by this giving, and themselves
made one with Them.

The soul that prays, begs this communication of the Spirit of
love. It asks God to give Himself to it. It then asks for what He
most desires. Between this infinite desire of God and the soul's
prayer there is a consonance, a harmony, a perfect understanding.
The humble soul recognizes that it has not in itself that desire, essentially divine, to give itself; that it can have it only if Love Himself gives it. The soul's humility thus touches the heart of God and
gives Him the glory He wants more than anything else. That is
why humility is all-powerful: it is irresistible. Before that prayer
He yields, He is moved, He is (dare I say so?) conquered — conquered by Himself, of course, by that very love, that very need to
give Himself, to which our humble prayer appeals.

The examples of this all-powerful humility are undoubtedly
very impressive. Jesus, as is only fitting, heads the list, with His
poor, broken body, His face covered with spittle, His whole being
shamefully treated and no longer human in its form.[79] Having become man, he is "despised of men." He has touched the lowest
depths of His abasement; "for which cause," says St. Paul, "God

[79] Cf. Isa. 53:2 ff.

also hath exalted Him, and hath given Him a name which is above all names."[80]

Then comes the humble Virgin: "Because He hath regarded the humility of His handmaid."[81] Thus she spoke of Him who had made her the Mother of God. It was her humility that He saw and loved and heard in her, and it is what He looks for and loves in us; it is what draws and constrains Him in our regard.

This "looking" of God at the soul that humbles itself in His presence, communicating eternal light and infinite love to it — what sweetness it brings to the soul in prayer, what strength. It was this that comforted the Canaanite woman at the feet of our Savior,[82] and the centurion in search of a miracle.[83] Jesus heard their prayer, which wrested from Him, as if by sheer force, both the miracle they sought and His delighted admiration.

The humble soul that prays presents itself with the attractive power of emptiness to the Being who is longing to fill it. There is no resistance to break, no other presence to dispel, no transformation to effect. He has only to enter, to take possession, to respond fully to the soul's yearnings. The "humble man" referred to in the text of St. James is the "poor man" of whom the psalmist is always speaking and mentioned in other parts of the Scriptures. God's wealth is His own, not because of a narrow and loveless justice, but because of the very profound nature of God Himself, who is love. "God is infinitely generous," says William of Auvergne.[84]

[80] Phil. 2:9.
[81] Luke 1:48.
[82] Matt. 15:22 ff.
[83] Matt. 8:5 ff.
[84] William of Auvergne (d. 1249), Bishop of Paris, philosopher, and theologian.

The Prayer of the Presence of God

"He loves to give as much as He is. He is never so happy as when He is giving Himself thus. Whoever tells Him of needs to be satisfied, of a weakness to be relieved, of sufferings to be healed, delights Him."

Chapter 25

Pray with your heart

There are no sterile prayers; there are only dried-up souls. The prayer of a dried-up soul is not a prayer; it is not a raising up of the mind to God. Such a soul is not living in God's presence, on His heights. It remains preoccupied with itself and might well die in that state. Only the lips mutter words, which could be prayers; or the arms are outstretched in a gesture that could be mistaken for one intended for God. But there is nothing of spiritual depth accompanying these external manifestations, which are deceptive. "With their lips [they] glorify me, but their heart is far from me."[85]

Nothing displeases God more than such a deception. Elsewhere He calls it "absolutely execrable," and that I understand. This particular lie destroys human integrity; it gives to the body and soul, which are substantially one, two divergent movements. By it we are debased lower than our real selves. St. Augustine compared it to the lowing of cattle, but even that is an understatement. A lowing is the cry of a beast. Prayer that is feigned is the word of a being divided in himself and reduced to a dried-up shell; it is not the prayer of a man.

The prayer of a proud man is not much better.

[85] Isa. 29:13.

The Prayer of the Presence of God

Such was the prayer of the Pharisee in the Temple.[86] He was not looking at God; he was looking at himself, and he expected God to do the same. The meek and humble Savior's condemnation of this Pharisee is well known. It showed all too clearly what our Lord thought of such an attitude, which the commentators on the Gospel do not always make enough of. Our Lord's words were devastating: "I say to you: this man [the publican] went down to his house justified, rather than the other [the Pharisee]."[87] The prayer of the Pharisee followed the line of his thought. He assumed a place of preference on earth and seemed to think he would occupy the same in Heaven. The contrast between him and the publican, the only representative of the human race present, showed up his superiority. Jesus took up the comparison, but, with one word, turned the tables on the proud Pharisee. But what a word. . . . He is now simply one who knew not how to achieve his being by freeing himself from himself and entering into the truth of God. "You thought you were rich and had need of nothing, and knew not that you were wretched and miserable, poor and blind and naked."[88]

Yet humility is not diffidence. On the contrary, it is the very opposite. Humility is so fine a combination that it is not easy to define it exactly. Perhaps the best definition of it is that it is the same as truth. Humility is an equation; it is a just relationship, perceived, accepted, and loved of the reality. And that reality is that God is essential being, whereas we exist only in Him. The soul that keeps in this place (that is, remains in the presence of Being Himself) in order that Being Himself may communicate His own life to it and thus cause it to be, is true and consequently humble.

[86] Luke 18:10.
[87] Luke 18:14.
[88] Cf. Apoc. 3:17 (RSV = Rev. 3:17).

Since the Fall, the truth is that man no longer lives in God's presence; he has turned away from Him, and only God can turn him back. The prayer of a diffident soul speaks only half that truth. It forgets the other half, so important and so comforting. Such a soul, says St. James, is "like a wave of the sea, which is moved and carried about by the wind."[89] God cannot impress His likeness upon it; it is not the perfect mirror in which He can reproduce and so give birth to His Son in us. What we must do when we pray is to place ourselves at our Lord's feet, and like children say, "Our Father."

[89] James 1:6.

☞

Chapter 26

Be sorry for your sins

The heart is not the same as sensitivity, except in its higher stage, that of reason. It is good to distinguish between them. The heart of an animal is sensitive; it has plenty of "heart" in that sense. But the man who has no other heart has not a heart at all! With all our knowledge today, we fail to appreciate this. We confuse the very inferior animal impressionability with that sensitivity which is essential to the real man, whom only truth and good, justice and beauty can move.

Compunction is that which pierces a man's heart when he remembers and reflects on these great realities, and especially on the greatest of realities: God. It takes on different forms and can have different causes.

The use of the word should be restricted really to the heart's sorrow at the thought or memory of sin, above all of our own sins. But it can also be applied to lively impressions felt at the sins of others, or at the possibility of committing sin. We feel compunction when we realize the grave consequences sin can have; when we think of our Lord's Passion, which blotted out our sins; of the presence within us of God giving Himself and preserving us from evil; of the hope of our future union with Him in our true homeland; or of the pain at seeing our exile, separating us from Him, prolonged.

The Prayer of the Presence of God

The effect is the same in any case, except for slight differences that we alone can perceive. That is because the ultimate cause is the same — namely, love. Whatever form it takes — regret, desire, hope, or joy — compunction is always the fruit of divine love; it is marked by the same characteristics and has, in God's eyes, the merit of that love. In compunction God sees the love that emanates from His divine heart communicating itself to our heart, and returning whence it came, enriched by all our heart has loved. True and really supernatural compunction is a very special grace. It can come only with a genuine and rare understanding of God, of His greatness and His beauty, of His love and our relations with Him, and from the joy of a life upheld by these relations. A soul that has received this understanding must possess a transparency that only a long life of loving detachment can obtain for it.

The Church Fathers have praised this grace in the highest terms. "Humble tears of the heart," wrote St. Jerome,[90] "you are a queen and all-powerful. You fear not the tribunal of the judge, and your presence silences those who accuse you. Nothing holds you back or keeps you from having access to the throne of grace, and never do you turn away with empty hands. The agony you cause the Devil is even worse than the pains of Hell. You triumph over the Unconquerable One; you bind and force the hand of the Almighty. Prayer alone can touch Him and, when that prayer is accompanied by tears of compunction, then it is irresistible. Prayer is oil that disposes God to listen; tears of compunction wound Him and oblige Him to act."

"The angels," says St. Bernard,[91] "are deeply moved by our tears of compunction, and by our holy prayers. For them, they are like a

---

[90] St. Jerome (c. 342-420), Doctor who translated the Bible into Latin.

[91] St. Bernard of Clairvaux (1090-1153), abbot and Doctor.

wine that intoxicates; they see in them the perfume of a true life assured by divine grace, the savor of the forgiveness of sins; the strong vigor of innocence recovered; the joy of reconciliation with God and the serene peace of a conscience again set in order."

"It is the fat and abundant holocaust of victims beloved of God," says St. Gregory.[92] "The heart's tears sprinkle it with the perfume He prefers before all others."

And St. John Climacus: "Tears lend wings to prayers, which fly straight to the heart of God."

Clearly tears of the kind referred to here are not necessarily actual tears, as shallow souls might think. Such souls work up a kind of excitement; their imagination dwells on those things that move them. They are glad when they can call forth tears; they appraise their love by this external, and sometimes childish, sign. What these Fathers are referring to are the genuine tears of the heart, which can easily be smothered by the effort to produce what is merely their external sign. What they have in mind is a wholly internal and spiritual movement that only the Spirit of love can excite in us, and we must ask Him for it with full confidence and then quietly await it. It is a clear and pure flame, which suddenly leaps up as from a hidden brazier. It lights up the mind and touches the chords of the heart. It moves the soul to its depths, causing a kind of heavenly thrill to pass through it, which lifts it up above itself, so that it exclaims, "My God," in a way which is altogether new to it. Then the distance separating it from Him who thus makes Himself known; the memory of its sins, which were responsible for that gulf; Jesus on the Cross expiating our sins, with Mary standing at His feet; Hell punishing the sin without relieving it of

---

[92] St. Gregory the Great (d. 604), Pope from 590, writer, and Doctor.

its debt — all these thoughts suddenly welling up before our eyes, ceasing to be thoughts and having become images: all this compresses the soul like a ripe fruit, causing the sweet and intoxicating tears to flow.

These tears, however, are not the end. The soul that weeps looks higher than its own self. It longs to attain the heights and already sees something of what it can and must attain. Nevertheless, it remains enclosed within the circle of its self, enlarged it is true, but still restrained and not destroyed. The Holy Spirit, who wants to set it free, prepares the soul for the final rapture, which is its determined end. God wants the soul entire; He wants to free it from itself and from created objects and raise it to Himself. Then the tears, tiny bouquets to cheer us on the way, cease, and the soul tastes in anticipation the joys of Heaven. The gift of tears is always a most precious gift. We should desire it, ask for it, and prepare ourselves for it. We must desire and ask for it with an assurance, a profound and lively conviction that God wishes to give it to us much more strongly than we can wish for it ourselves. We can be sure that our desire, however exalted we may be, is no more than a tiny spark in God's immense desire to grant it to us.

Chapter 27

ᡣ

Reflect on what Christ
suffered because of sin

We must have the courage to look often at the horrible thing we call sin, as it actually is in the light of truth. Sin is a direct, violent, deliberate, and maybe mortal blow given to Love within us, in order to get rid of Him and put ourselves in His place. We must see this horrible thing becoming the daily nourishment of so many souls, who lap it up like water, establishing itself as master in a world that owes its very existence, and its continued existence, to that Love we crucify.

We must stand before that Love on the Cross. He is a living Person, a man of three and thirty years and in the prime of life; endowed with an incomparable wealth of sensitiveness. He possesses a heart and mind of extreme delicacy. Heaven and earth, Creator and creature, the finite and the infinite are united in Him — all rights, all greatness, all truth, and all good; all that can call for admiration, respect, sympathy, and love. For thirty years He has been ignored, and very possibly persecuted. For three years, men have envied Him, attacked Him, and done their best to hinder His good works. For three hours of profound agony, He has borne in His filial soul the weight of the anger of His Father, whom man has offended. For twelve hours, His poor body has been beaten, broken in every sense, and under every form, and His heart reflects all the sufferings of His beloved friends gathered around Him, whose pain but increases His own. Finally, when He is completely at the end of His strength, of His life's blood, His honor and His love, His Father, who remained to Him His sole help, would seem to have forsaken Him. This, indeed, is the final blow. Then, at last, "it is finished."[93]

The debt of man's sin is paid, but at what a price! It is the price of a soul delivered up to wicked men. "We grieve," says St. Augustine, "over a soul abandoned by its body; but what sort of Christian feelings have we, not to grieve for a soul separated from God?"

St. Augustine is right to denounce our want of spiritual sensitiveness. But he knows what we lack and how to obtain it — he who so long wept for his own sins. What we lack is the light of that Love, which makes us see our sins in their frightening truth, as God sees them. To obtain this light, we must ask for it and wait. It does not always come all at once when we ask for it, but it will, sooner or later, come to those who know how to wait.

93 John 19:30.

Part 3

Growing Closer to God

Chapter 28

Prepare yourself to pray

Prayer is, as it were, being alone with God. A soul prays only when it is turned toward God, and for so long as it remains so. As soon as it turns away, it stops praying. The preparation for prayer is thus the movement of turning to God and away from all that is not God. That is why we are so right when we define prayer as this movement. Prayer is essentially a "raising up," an elevation. We begin to pray when we detach ourselves from created objects and raise ourselves up to the Creator.

Now, this detachment is born when we clearly realize our nothingness. That is the real meaning of our Lord's words: "He that shall humble himself shall be exalted."[94] His whole life was a continual abasement, always more and more profound. St. Bernard does not hesitate to say that such an abasement brings us face-to-face with God. Hence the peace of souls that have fallen, when, raised up by God, they find themselves in His presence. And it is precisely in their abasement, once they have recognized and admitted it, that they find Him, because it is there that He reveals Himself. The only thing that prevents Him from doing so is our "self." When we own to our nothingness, this "self" is broken down, and once that happens, the mirror is pure, and God can produce His

[94] Matt. 23:12.

own image in the soul, which then faithfully reproduces His features that are revealed in all their harmony and perfect beauty.

This is what our Lord meant in that vital passage in the Sermon on the Mount, and what all human considerations on prayer repeat endlessly but without arriving at its full splendor: "But thou, when thou shalt pray, enter into thy chamber and, having shut the door, pray to thy Father in secret."[95] Enter this sacred chamber of your soul and there, having closed the door, speak to your Father, who sees you in these secret depths, and say to Him, "Our Father, who art in Heaven. . . ." This intimate presence; your faith in Him who *is* the secret depth of it and gives Himself there; the silence toward all that is not God in order to be all to Him — here is the preparation for prayer.

It is obvious that we do not reach such a state of soul without being prepared for it by quite a combination of circumstances. And this is just what we do not know sufficiently in practice. The way to prepare for prayer is by leading a divine life, and prayer, after all, is that divine life. Everything that reproduces God's image in us; everything that raises us beyond and above created things; every sacrifice that detaches us from them; every aspect of faith that reveals the Creator to us in creatures; every movement of true and disinterested love making us in unison with the Three in One — all this is prayer and prepares us for a still more intimate prayer. All this makes real the divine word of the Sermon on the Mount and the dual movement it recommends: *shut the door* and *pray to thy Father*. When He spoke thus, the divine Word showed that He knew our being and its laws. He revealed Himself as our Creator and made Himself our Redeemer. He showed that He made us and that He alone can remake us.

[95] Matt. 6:6.

We do not suffice to ourselves; we have not in us that which can complete us; we need to be completed. I know I am putting it badly when I say that this complementing thing is not in us. Actually, it is in within us, but it is in a part of us that is, as it were, outside of us. In us, as in God, there are "many mansions."[96] God is within us in the depths of our soul, but by sin we no longer occupy those depths. When Eve looked at the forbidden fruit and stretched out her hand to take it and eat it, she went out of those secret depths in her soul. It was these depths that were the real terrestrial paradise, where God visited our first parents and spoke to them. Since the Fall, God is in us, but we are not!

The preparation for prayer consists in returning to those depths. Renunciation, detachment, recollection — whatever word we use, the reality is the same, and that reality is the true secret of prayer. *Close the door* and *enter.* . . . It needs only these two phrases to explain this, but in reality they are only one thing. They represent a movement, for all that unites us to God is movement. The words are related to two "terms," or ends. If we speak of the *terminus a quo* (that is, *from*), they say (and they do what they say): *Close.* If we think of the *terminus ad quem* (that is, *to*), they say: *Enter.* We have to close the door on all that is not, and enter into HIM WHO IS. There you have the secret of all prayer.

---

[96] John 14:2.

Chapter 29

⌒

Enter your "inner chamber"

God is a brazier of love. Prayer brings us near to Him, and in coming near to Him, we are caught by His fire. The soul is raised by the action of this fire, which is a kind of spiritual breath that spiritualizes it and carries it away. The soul frees itself from all that weighs it down, keeping it attached to this wearisome earth. The psalmist compares this breath to incense.[97] Now, incense is a symbol universally known and exceptionally rich. But from all the substances that fire penetrates under the form of flame or heat, there follows a movement by which it spreads, causing it to increase by communicating itself to all that surrounds it.

The movement of the soul that prays has something special about it. It goes out from itself and yet remains in itself. It passes from its natural state to its supernatural state; from itself in itself to itself in God. At first glance, these expressions may seem strange. The mystery is not in the realities but in our understanding of them. Our mind is not used to these realities; we have to become accustomed to them.

Our soul is a dwelling with many apartments. In the first, it is there with the body; that is to say, with all the body's sensitiveness.

[97] Cf. Ps. 140:2 (RSV = Ps. 141:2): "Let my prayer be directed as incense in Thy sight."

95

The Prayer of the Presence of God

It sees when the eye sees, hears when the ear hears. It moves with the muscles; it remembers, imagines, and appreciates distances, when we take part in all the activities that are the common ground of its action with the body. In the second, the soul is alone and acts alone. The body is there — it is always there — but it no longer acts; it has no part in the soul's action. The soul alone thinks and loves. The body with its senses prepares the matter and elements, the conditions of this spiritual activity, but it has no part in producing it. That room is closed; the soul is there alone and dwells there alone.

In that spiritual dwelling there is a part still more remote. It is the dwelling-place of being, who communicates Himself and makes us to "be." We are so accustomed to live turned outward (and objects of sense keep us so turned), we hardly ever open the door of that chamber, and scarcely give it a glance; many die without ever suspecting its existence. Men ask, "Where is God?" God is there — in the depths of their being — and He is there communicating being to them. They are not HIM WHO IS and who gives being to all other things. They receive being; they receive a part of being that does not depend upon themselves. They receive it for a certain time and under certain forms. And from His "beyond" God gives them existence. They exist only by His power and are only what He enables them to be. He is at the source of all they do and, no matter how much they may desire to continue those activities, they cannot do so if He is not there. To understand this, we have to think a great deal, and reflection — perhaps the highest form human act can take — has given place to exterior action and to local movement, both of which are common to animals and matter.

The soul that prays enters into this upper room. It places itself in the presence of that Being who gives Himself, and it enters into communication with Him. To *communicate* means to have something in common and, by this common element, to be made one. We touch, we speak, we open out to one another. Without this "something," we remain at a distance; we do not "communicate." God is love. We enter into communication with Him when we love, and in the measure of our love. The soul that loves and that has been introduced by Love into that dwelling-place where Love abides can speak to Him. Prayer is that colloquy. God will not resist that love which asks. He has promised to do the will of those who do His will.[98]

It is to love that is due these divine communications which have drawn from those happy recipients the most amazing exclamations. "Lord, stay, I beg you, the torrent of your love. I can bear no more." The soul, submerged and ravished, has fainted under the weight of these great waters and has asked to be allowed to take breath for an instant, in order the better to renew its welcome. The anchorite in the desert, when he prayed, had to forbear extending his arms, so as not to be rapt in his prayer. St. Mary the Egyptian, St. Francis of Assisi, were raised up from the ground and remained upheld by a power greater than the weight of their body.[99]

[98] Cf. Ps. 144:19 (RSV = Ps. 145:19): "He will do the will of them that fear Him."
[99] St. Mary the Egyptian (c. 344-c. 421), penitent and hermit; St. Francis of Assisi (1182-1226), founder of the Franciscan Order.

Chapter 30

⁀

Rejoice in God's attentiveness to you

The saints have written wonderful pages on the theme of the divine friendship. "What dignity and what glory on the part of Almighty God," says St. John Chrysostom, "to be ever attentive to listen to us."

Weak creatures, poor beings of a day, tiny flowers born at dawn, only to fade by evening — we have but to turn to Him, and at once He gives us audience. He speaks to us, caresses us; He gives Himself. He stoops to our wretchedness and raises us up to His throne. He bid us enter His chamber — the chamber that is His love — the very movement of His being and life. I would tire the best of friends or the most leisured, were I to present myself thus at any hour. My unconstrained and easygoing manner would hurt the kindest of men. Yet God receives me always, and excuses and overlooks my lack of courtesy.

Not only does He receive me; He spoils me. He shows me the splendors of His palace. He has always some new light to offer to my mind, some delight to my heart. And should that light be one already known to me, He clothes it with the freshness of an early spring flower.

Should He think it necessary to leave me in darkness, that night becomes day, and the deepest shadows are transformed into the brightest light. And if He refuses me pleasures of the senses,

The Prayer of the Presence of God

He makes me find in the prayer of the desert superior delights that enchant my childlike faith in my Father.

These divine relations would suffice me a thousand times, if He presented Himself alone, for He is all, and all to me. But He is accompanied by a great and wondrous company. The greatest souls of all times, raised up and radiant with light that surrounds them, are there with Him, as loving and as good as He. They show me the same love; they offer to share with me their happiness, and the joy of their relations with HIM WHO IS and who gives Himself. They take my prayers before they have risen from my heart to my lips. They present them to God, enriched with their fraternal supplication; they impart to them the perfume of their smile. They add to them their own merits.

In such company we forget the earth; we no longer think of men and their littlenesses (and our own); we forget all that depresses or saddens us. We become serene and almost in Heaven. We feel great, strong, and consoled.

How the adversaries of our salvation appear despicable — and indeed they are! God, His grace, the virtues with which He fortifies and ennobles us; the eternal happiness that He promises and of which He occasionally gives us a foretaste; Heaven growing nearer and almost opening — all this can help us to forget the dangers and the hours of desolation of the way. Prayer brings the soul into the presence of these realities; indeed, more than into their presence, for we actually enter the divine presence-chamber.

"Prayer," says St. John Climacus, "unites us to God, sustains the world, renders souls beautiful, blots out sin, preserves us from temptation, and defends us in the time of battle. It consoles us when the storm breaks, is the mother of fertile tears, and changes tears of regret into tears of love. It feeds our spiritual joys, and nourishes our activities which give birth to them. The perfect virtues, the higher graces, the delights of hearts transformed and made one in God, the most profound lights, the quiet feeling of security and assured hopes, the great progress of souls and the striking divine interventions — all depend upon prayer.

Chapter 31

⌒

Let prayer bring
peace to your soul

Between the development of prayer and the elevation of souls, there exists an assured connection, universally admitted, which is essential. In being raised up, the soul arrives at regions untouched by the agitation of transitory things. All movement ceases or grows less. The passions are calmed, the noise of the world, its cares, even our thoughts fade into the distance, and our attention is concentrated on Him alone who is silence, repose, and the God of peace. We feel invaded by calm and, as it were clothed, in the divine immutability, which seems to communicate itself to our whole being. This is where prayer flourishes — that prayer which is a devout upsurge of love, which draws us toward God, who is unceasingly inclined toward us. His Spirit enfolds us, penetrates us, descends into our depths, and says, "My son. . . ." Then, returning from the depths of our being, which he turns back to its Source, he answers for us: "Father."[100] There is no greater or more profound moment, no higher activity possible.

In a soul praying thus, certain dispositions are necessary, requiring long exercise and sustained effort. Our sensitiveness, distorted as a result of the Fall, rebels. It alternates between mad

[100]Gal. 4:6.

outbreaks and periods of discouragement. It does not want to take up its role of servant; it wants to be its own master, to follow its own caprices. And so it resists. Any opposition infuriates it. The more we try to discipline it, the more it throws off all restraint and goes mad. We have to re-orientate it, restore it to its proper place, which is that of a servant — useful but submissive. The wrecked harmony of the fine human edifice that God made must be re-established. We do not realize enough that He alone can do this. The absolute necessity for His aid is about the last idea to enter into our heads and persuade us to turn to Him. We spend the whole of our lives trying to sanctify ourselves without His help, and we are convinced that we can manage it of ourselves.

Properly understood and well carried out, prayer restores us to our position as a creature receiving all from the Creator. Without His aid we are not only weak, but completely helpless. Now we see clearly again and unmistakably; we see what we have to do, and we can do it, for God who is Truth is in us, and He is giving Himself. Hitherto, we were in our nothingness and were content to remain there. The soul that prays might still be far from perfect, but it is on its way and it will arrive at perfection. It is united with the Source who will give it that perfection. It will welcome the knowledge of what it should do moment by moment. It follows a way that is sure, for this way is also the end. The soul is both traveling to that end and has at the same time arrived at it. God Himself prays in that soul, leads it to Him, and already gives Himself to it.

Prayer proceeds from union; it seeks it and attains it. God is continually making us ask for what He wants to give us, and He gives what He makes us ask for. Then He inscribes this movement in His Book of Life; the angels record it and, delighted, treasure every single note of it. They seize them before the lips utter them, sometimes barely or badly formed, seeing only the right intention or the frailty which is our excuse. "Prayer," says St. Augustine, "serves the needs of souls, and draws down the help they seek; delights the angels, infuriates Hell, and is to God a sacrifice that cannot but be pleasing to Him. It is the crowning point of religion, the unspoilt praise, the perfect glory, and the source of the most assured hope."

How is it possible to prefer vain discourses, wasted hours, stupid amusements, and pointless dreams to such joy, such a treasure, and so great an honor? God is there. He awaits us, He calls us; He offers us enlightenment for our mind, strength for our will, unspeakable joys for our sensitive nature, and priceless treasures for ourselves and others. And we turn our backs on Him!

We have our excuse, it is true — it is His very love, ceaselessly offering itself and apparently eager to give itself. But the gift of oneself appears degrading only to sordid souls. Noble souls know that this love He offers us is the truth and the life, and they love to be held by this Love, who reveals Himself and, in doing, so gives Himself.

Chapter 32

⌒

Develop a filial
relationship with God

Here I am repeating myself again! And yet I am not afraid of tiring myself or of displeasing the One I seek in these extravagant efforts of my unsatisfied mind. I have not said enough about the extent to which the soul that prays must believe in the love of the God to whom it prays. Yes, prayer is like speaking face-to-face with God. God and the soul are on the same level; they occupy the same inner chamber. They are like Father and son, the Spouse and his bride, like Friend and friend. The soul's colloquy with God must, then, have one essential characteristic: intimacy, an intimacy born of the closest family ties. The child sees and loves with the light and love of the Father; he sees what the Father sees. He does not see all that the Father sees, but he sees all that the Father enables him to see. He is happy in that union accorded him by the Father, by which the Father makes him His son, for this union is truly the communication of His own divine life.

This unshakable confidence in the God who is Love, in the Father giving Himself to souls, is all-powerful. "If you shall have faith . . . and shall say to this mountain, 'Take up and cast thyself into the sea,' it shall be done." [101] "They that trust in Him shall

[101] Matt. 21:21.

understand the truth, and they that are familiar in love shall rest in Him."[102] "Be of good heart. . . . Thy faith hath made thee whole."[103] These are actual assurances from the Spirit of love; they are beyond question and leave no room for doubt.

This confidence goes very far; it must allow no trial and no delay to affect it. "Although He should kill me," says Job, "I will trust in Him."[104] It must hold the difficult golden mean between presumption (which would suppress all human effort) and doubt (which, having made the effort, does not really believe in the all-powerfulness of the God who is love or in the love of the all-powerful God).

All the other conditions required by the prayer of faith lead more or less to those I have suggested. The ardent love of the poor sinner to whom Jesus said, "Many sins are forgiven her, because she hath loved much"[105]; that collective prayer which He assures us is all-powerful with His Father;[106] those works of mercy which undoubtedly call down the divine blessing on those who perform them;[107] the generous pardon extended to those who have offended against us[108] — this is what the Holy Spirit is glad to find in the souls of those who appeal to His love. So, too, is the conversion of heart that restores us once more to the favor of the good God;[109] the recognition of our plight, which suffices to keep us in

[102]Wisd. 3:9.
[103]Matt. 9:22.
[104]Job 13:15.
[105]Luke 7:47.
[106]Matt. 18:19.
[107]Cf. Matt. 25:40.
[108]Matt. 18:22.
[109]Cf. Ps. 50:14 (RSV = Ps. 51:12).

the light and truth;[110] the asking again and again, which is evidence of our determined confidence;[111] our patience in times of trial and our solicitude for the divine glory[112] — it is in such human voices as these that God recognizes His own voice and responds to it.

---

[110]Cf. Ps. 50:5 (RSV = Ps. 5:31).
[111]Cf. Matt. 21:22.
[112]Cf. 1 Cor. 10:31.

Chapter 33

☞

Meet God in the
silence of your soul

We have to accustom ourselves to pray in all places as at all times. The real place to pray in is the soul, for God dwells there. If we wish to obey our Lord's counsel, when we pray we should enter the chamber of our soul, close the door, and speak to the Father, whose loving eyes seek ever our own.[113] This inner chamber of our soul is the true temple, the sacred sanctuary, and we carry it with us and can at any time either remain there or quickly return to it, should we have been obliged to leave it.

And we must make it a really spotless and beautiful place. Its true beauty, of course, is our Lord's presence. In it He should be able to feel at home, and He is at home if He sees His own features there. These features are His perfections, and when they are reflected in the soul, they are called *virtues*. The soul that possesses them is beautiful with His beauty; it is perfect "as our heavenly Father is perfect."[114] The *as* here does not mean "as much"; it does not imply equality but resemblance. By the virtues we are reformed in God's image, and in the image of His divine Son, who came to reveal His Father's features to us, by practicing the virtues.

[113]Matt. 6:6.
[114]Cf. Matt. 5:48.

The Prayer of the Presence of God

In this reserved sanctuary — a new heaven and kingdom of God — solitude and silence must reign. God is alone with Himself. The divine Persons do not affect this solitude; they constitute it. The Love who is their animating force encloses them against all that is not Himself. The City of God is immense, but enclosed. God alone occupies it, and He is *All in all*. The soul that prays must reproduce this solitude; it must be filled by it to the exclusion of all else. The very colloquy that follows is a kind of silence.

Speech and silence are not opposed; they do not exclude one another. What is opposed to silence is not speech but words — that is, multiplicity. We confuse the silence of being with the silence of "nothingness," which knows neither how to speak nor how to be silent. All that it can do is to become agitated, and then it dissembles. And it does this by its superficial movements reflecting the nothingness within it. Lip service, which has no deep thought to support it; physical posturings; facial expressions with no corresponding reality or that flatly deceive — such is the language of "nothingness."

And that is why it is garrulous. It says little in many words; or it uses words that do not say what it thinks. God needed only one Word to express Himself fully, and it is toward that unity (of the Word) that we tend when we are alone with God. He has become all, and we tell Him so — what more can we say? It is the silence of the soul recollected in itself and occupied with Him whom it finds there. It is the silence of those long nights that Jesus passed on the mountainside during His prayer to God. It was the silence of Gethsemane or of Calvary, broken only by a few words for us.

Churches are places for prayer in common. They must reproduce God's features and those of souls that need the body to express themselves. They must offer to the body lines that run upward toward Heaven or fade away in the mystery of a semidarkness.

They must isolate the building from the world and its noises, and form a central point around which everything tends to draw the soul's powers, to concentrate and unify them and evoke our love. They must reveal beauties that are altogether beyond us; they must give us a peace that does not come from created things but draws us above them. They must create a great harmony of the natural and the supernatural, in which He who has made both matter and spirit is revealed. His presence shines through, and His love draws us. We must breathe Him through the very pores of our being, just as we breathe the air. A place of worship that does not evoke this response, and the soul that, on entering it, does not respond to that appeal are not true to themselves and deceive others.

Chapter 34

⌒

Speak to God as a child to his father

Formal prayers are in general directives that are suitable to all souls and for all times. They are models, so to speak, ready made. Our customary morning and evening prayers are good examples. These formal prayers are not useless. How many souls would, without them, put themselves into the presence of God, and confide in Him? Of ourselves, we know neither what to say nor how to say it.[115]

What, then, are these formal prayers? What is their theme or, better, their essential themes? What must we say to God when we approach Him, so that His fatherly love may be awakened and His ear be ready to listen to us? What must we say so that contact may be established, without which no prayer is possible?

There are two ideas that govern all our relations with Him. In all circumstances, they must be found at the bottom of all our prayers. They are their beginning, their development, and their conclusion. Prayers can take place in the one, but the other is more or less implied. If it is not, then it is not true prayer. For whoever prays truly, God is always HE WHO IS, infinite being, whose majesty is beyond all conception. His wisdom is infinite, His power infinite, and His love inexpressible. Everything proceeds from Him; all

[115]Cf. Mark 10:38; Jer. 1:6.

things are in His hands. When He commands, nothing can resist Him. All that He wills, is; all that opposes His designs are made to serve their very purpose. He punishes every fault and rewards every merit. His eye, either stern or encouraging, follows all we do, aids all our efforts, sustains our weaknesses, and rectifies our mistakes.

We must never tire of telling Him this. Such constant repetition delights Him and is excellent: it could not be better. It puts God in His place, and us in ours. By acknowledging to Him what He is, we remind Him of what we are — nothingness in revolt. To recognize this is an immense grace, and is the result of His light in us. When we see ourselves in that light, it is because He is there, and our mind welcomes His light. There we are no longer "nothing" or in revolt; we are children of light. He has reproduced His Son in us, and thus tastes the joy of being a Father. Our soul is His abiding place, and we abide in Him. Those intimate relations that the saints tell us of take place in the serene depths of a heart even when it is forgetful of Him and is stained by sin. These relations can go on developing and can even attain to exchanges of love that no earthly language can describe, and which are already the beginning of eternity. "Heaven is in my soul, for Heaven is God, and God is in my soul." On that double theme — the loving greatness of God and the loved nothingness of the creature — we can go on meditating indefinitely, and we should do so.

First, we should profit by formal prayers in common use. They lead each heart to express itself after its own fashion. Then, little by little, with practice, we learn to rely on them less and less as interpreters; we need them less when we have learned to speak the same language. Indeed, occasionally, they can impart too formal a character when those relations develop a more intimate strain. Yet such prayers, ready formed, can sometimes be necessary or even useful, since God is always in a sense a "stranger" to us. "He came unto His own, and His own received Him not."[116] The gentle pace, the freedom of family conversation in which we go from one subject to another or express ourselves in half-phrases, are perhaps better. Our looks speak for us; a smile or a gesture can say more than any word could do. A kiss begins and ends everything — if we can speak of a beginning and an end in such matters.

My tongue runs away with me when I begin thinking of these things. Without my being aware of it, my mind turns again to the subject I love: the filial and simple prayer of interior souls. To these God says in the depths of their being, "You are my beloved child. I am here. Let us talk." To a child whose soul has awakened with the sweet image of His Father loving him more than an earthly father; present in his soul, as the soul of his soul and communicating His life to him, to whom he can speak without constraint, surrounded by the tenderness such as one finds in a true home — the simple and easy conversation with this Father would be like the movement and respiration of the heart, and his whole life would be a prayer.

[116]John 1:11.

Chapter 35

Remember that God acts for your good

We make too many distinctions; it is the fault of our present way of thinking. Justice and mercy are not two distinct realities, but only two distinct ideas that meet in one and the same reality: love.

In God's presence, we act as a son used to do in days gone by in the presence of his father. The father was in every sense the head of the family and exercised his rights as such. His love was the same as a father's love today (perhaps more so), but he knew that to love means wanting what is good for one's offspring, not just what is pleasant. In order to obtain this good, which was his sole aim, he knew how to command, how to impose his will, to check caprices, to direct and discipline energies, to prune the false shoots — in a word, he knew how to make a man of his son. If firmness was necessary, he was firm; if punishment was called for, he punished. He warned, scolded, and commanded, according to the needs of the moment, since his son was, as it were, a prolongation of himself, and continued to be so for a long time. He truly represented the Creator, so far as his child was concerned, and like the Creator, he combined justice with love.

In correcting he loved, and he corrected by love. And his son understood this and responded to that true love with a profound tenderness. And the more he received of that communication of life, the more he began to resemble his father and became a true son; and the more a friendship and intimacy sprang up between them. The son received more confidences and was encouraged to render little services. And so, little by little, he was initiated by concrete examples and acts rather than by words, to fulfill his future role as a father and head, thereby assuring in him the continuity of the family.

God acts in much the same way in our regard. He makes us in His image, thus acting as a Father with all a father's love. He employs for this purpose all sorts of means. Justice is one. The child must admit his faults, accept remonstrances, and learn by them to grow in love; to understand that love and the need to communicate life demand and call for reproofs. Under that discipline, he grows up and gradually takes a greater part in the life of his father. He acts more like his father yet remains more truly a son, more one of the family.

At the same time, he is entrusted with the secrets, the care, and the hopes of the family life, and thus becomes the friend, the companion, the future father. The Holy Spirit shows him souls, sometimes near to him, sometimes far away. They may be only a few, or they may be mankind in general. The Spirit reveals to him their needs, the ills from which they suffer, and the effort required to lead them back to their Father's home. And so his prayer becomes more catholic and universal. His gaze, lit up by the divine light, embraces the whole world. All kinds of feelings fill his soul, and love is the center, with all the shades of which it is capable. He still sees God as Someone very great, and himself as nothing. But between that Love and that "nothing" have been set in motion such relations that they speak the same language and present the same features. This prayer is true prayer, and there is nothing higher.

Chapter 36

Strive for a proper attitude of soul

Before arriving at these heights and even afterward, prayer can present, in turn, the various aspects that finally constitute it. The filial soul, very docile, accepts them by degrees and in the measure in which the Spirit of the Father communicates them to it.

Sometimes it sees the judge clearly, fathoming the recesses of its heart and its days, and revealing to it all the wretchedness with which life is always more or less filled. Its selfishness and sensuality, its pride and vanity, its jealousy and feelings of spite, its violence and cowardice, its foolish enthusiasms, fears, and indolence — all pass one by one in its thought, or gather together into one frightening picture. Then again, it finds itself in the presence of the Creator, communicating to it all that it has of being and life. It sees Him by faith, present in His own depths, imparting to it that life which unites them. It knows that it is made by Him, that it comes from Him, is united to Him, and is, as it were, filled and inundated by Him.

It also sees Him in all created things. All the earth is the work of His hands; all creation comes from Him and from Him alone. Beyond the visible world, His immensity spreads itself within itself, proceeding from Him alone and perfected in Him alone. He is alone, unique, independent, immutable, eternal; the source of all intelligence and of all goodness; remaining within Himself, while giving Himself; spreading Himself, so to say, without increasing His greatness. Before this — for we must always come back to this — our mind halts, stunned and dazed, and our heart is gently drawn to Him.

Again, the Spirit of Jesus, the incarnate Son of God, murmurs only one word: *Father.* The soul feels a slight breath pass through it, the breath of the divine life that the Father communicates eternally to the Son. At this breath, the soul feels turned around, powerfully drawn and carried up to Him who is giving Himself to it. The Spirit raises up the soul, takes it out of itself, breathes into it light and energies of which it is not aware. It wants to resemble, to take to itself and be united with that Spirit, who is the Spirit of God. It recalls the words of the Son of God in the Gospels: "Be ye perfect, as also your heavenly Father is perfect."[117] Or the word of God recorded in Leviticus: "Be holy because I am holy."[118] It understands that this reflection of the divine Beauty in it seems to make the Father grow greater, and gives Him joy and glory. It asks and wants that joy and glory for Him who imparts to it His life and the glorious light of His love.

It asks it for itself and for others, for the greatest number possible — for all men. It cannot understand why all men are not carried away and transformed by this desire. It calls them, invites them; it sings, "All ye works of the Lord, bless the Lord; praise and exalt Him above all forever. Earth exult, break out into cries of joyfulness; angels of Heaven, virtues of earth, stars of the firmament, zephyrs of the air, showers and dews, ice and snow, mountains and hills, waters and the sea, birds of the air and fish from the waters which animate them with their rapid motions; children of

[117]Matt. 5:48.
[118]Lev. 11:44.

men and the people of God, priests and devout servants of the
Most High — praise Him and bless Him; sing that He is great
above all these things; unite in that praise so that it fills the
Heaven and the earth, time and eternity, forever."[119]

Before this picture of the whole of creation praising and blessing, the Spirit shows the indifference and incomprehension of
men — souls that revolt and give voice to hatred instead of love.
We see divine Love despised and above all misunderstood. Under
the very eyes of the Father, crowds unnumbered are in danger of
being hurled into the abyss, insensible to His voice, to all the evidence of His love, to their own true interests. There are others
who pass long years before this spectacle, which for them becomes
living. It enters into their very soul and crushes and shatters them.
Jesus allows them to share, from afar, very afar, the hours of His agony in the Garden of Olives and His supreme abandonment on
Calvary. At the sight of these things, which crushes and overwhelms them, they perceive what a heart infinitely tender and
delicate — much more so than that of any mother, spouse, or
friend of all time — has had to suffer in these hours. There are
others whom the feeling of justice invades, fills, and raises up.
They ask, demand, and indeed insist on the punishment of so
many crimes. "My God," they say, "Your eyes are purity itself; they
cannot bear the sight of iniquity. How can You put up with those
who do evil, and keep silent when the wicked persecute the
just?"[120]

Again, there are some who no longer seem to see anything or
to wish for anything. They enter into a deep silence. For them
God is like a distant and hidden place of retreat. These souls

[119]Cf. Dan. 3:52 ff.
[120]Cf. Apoc. 6:10 (RSV = Rev. 6:10).

remain there with Him; they savor Him as one savors a ripe fruit. They listen to the beauty of His voice, and His words fill them with delights of which nothing can give any idea here below. An immense peace fills them, wraps them around, cradles them like a mother cradles her child. They seem to have crossed for an instant the threshold of the abode where one loves and is loved in the light and the truth, and they understand that to remain there is the true life. In this life, such a repose is short, such satisfaction rare. We must resume our journey and our effort; we must be resigned to continue our pilgrimage to our true home, like children loved but still in exile.[121]

These varying forms of prayer are all part of a deep unity. The same divine Breath inspires them, the same Love directs them, the same Word speaks to them, the same Father utters this word in the depths of their heart. Unity and distinction — divine characteristics marking all life like all being. It is the same God still giving Himself to souls, with the same love and in the various attitudes that He assumes in their regard when they pray.

This diversity of attitude is very strange, at least at first sight. Is it not opposed to love? Do we see the same kind of thing in the relations between a mother and her child, which is the nearest comparison we can get in the realm of human tenderness? Maternal affection and all human affections are comparisons, but only comparisons. They give us some idea of the reality, but they do not reproduce it wholly.

Further, we are guilty and sick souls. An erring child is still loved, but he has to be made to realize his fault, and if it is for his good, he must be punished. A sick child is surrounded by the most

[121]Cf. Heb. 11:13: "Confessing that they are pilgrims and strangers on earth." Cf. also 1 Pet. 2:11.

delicate attentions, but if a painful operation is necessary, the parents do not hesitate to agree to it. When we love, we want the good of the one we love, and all that can procure it. The various attitudes of God toward our prayers have no other explanation.

Chapter 37

⌒

Persist in prayer when God seems absent

That is why some souls of high virtue and ardent piety are submitted by God to the trial of aridity in prayer. The Holy Spirit, the divine Consoler, instead of invading them with this delightful sense of His tenderness, instead of speaking to them the sweet language of His love, of making them taste the joy of His presence, seems to draw back, to be silent, to leave them alone, abandoned to themselves. For a long time, as soon as they began to pray, they found Him there, they "felt" Him, they heard Him. A delightful and conscious intimacy sprang up between them. The soul forgot the world, it understood its vanity and emptiness; it withdrew from it and let fall one by one all the ties that could have held it back and prevented it from surrendering to the divine intimacy. God became for it every day more and more all, and everything else more and more nothing.

Then, suddenly, God withdraws Himself and leaves the soul alone and abandoned. The soul is without that world which it had given up for His sake, and without God, who should have replaced all that it had sacrificed. Only those who have loved and have concentrated their lives upon a single object can understand the awfulness of this loneliness and state of abandonment.

And often it becomes more complicated still, for God allows the enemy of mankind to profit by this apparent withdrawal, in order to launch more vigorous attacks on the soul. Sickness, persecutions, temptations, trials of every kind fall on the abandoned soul. Heaven seems to unite with earth to crush it, and prayer, the only resource left to it, seems to lose itself in the emptiness of its deserted heart. All around it, those who do not pray appear to be experiencing nothing but prosperity and joy. Everything succeeds with them. The Master they have forgotten overwhelms them with kindnesses, while they themselves insult Him. And He answers by heaping His rewards on them!

And the Devil takes advantage of these things and makes the most of these anomalies. He repeats the *why*. "Why," he insinuates, "why not give way and follow a way leading to these delights? Why remain faithful to a Master who is so feeble or so cruel?"

This Master often goes still further to test our love. To His silence and apparent abandonment of our soul, He is not afraid to add what seems to be discontent with us; He appears to be irritated and pitiless. He assumes a hostile appearance; He treats severely a love that has given up everything for His sake.

These are prayer's sublime moments, as sublime as they are hard. Faith, become the expression of charity, faith that has taken the name of confidence now sends its roots deep down whence will spring up the most marvelous results. To souls that are firm, that know how to pursue even to the depths of themselves the God who hides Himself there, He reserves fresh meetings and unsuspected intimacies. He withdraws, but only to entice the soul further. He wants to know, through the fire of this testing time, the reality and strength of the soul's love. He wants to draw it up into the regions of being far removed from the world, from nature, from all created things, so that it may never again fall back. He obliges the soul to burn its boats, to take to the waters, and so rejoin Him on the far side of the river. To love is to give oneself, to forget oneself.

Moreover, He is there all the time — He, the essential gift of self, secretly sustaining and, without our being aware of it, drawing us in a way more and more irresistible and delectable. The soul no longer recognizes Him and is unconscious of His action. But a new and greater assurance, of a kind more solid than ever, grows slowly like the first glimmer of the dawn in a night still dark; and the soul knows that the approaching day is bringing it closer to the truth and the life. This is not the same as its former happiness, but is a foretaste of a new happiness, to which is united the memory of past joys or the hope of deeper and purer joys to come.

And in this silence, the soul hears a voice. It is conscious of a presence in this solitude. It suspects a love in this abandonment and even in the apparent hostility, and in all this divine trial it sees the hand that is fashioning and remaking it more and more in the likeness of the divine Model.

Part 4

The Prayer of Praise

Chapter 38

＝

Let your praise be a foretaste of eternity

All prayer is praise. Even that of the publican beating his breast[122] is a hymn to the greatness of God. His prayer proclaimed God's merciful goodness, which is the very summit of that greatness. The Love who raised up mankind after the Fall is the same Love rewarding the soul in the evening of its struggles. To ask God for His help is to proclaim His power. Nevertheless it would appear to be the custom to reserve this title of praise to the hymn of those for whom the combat has ceased, either because they have retired from the fray and have entered into their eternal rest, or because they are joined to the Master in such a way that they have found in Him their place of repose.[123] Having nothing further to fear or to ask for, and their transformation being complete, they have now only to live according to that new form which is a participation in the divine life.[124] Their only activity henceforth is to rest in the indescribable joy which is having their being from Him, for Him, by Him, and in Him. This joy is their prayer.

[122]Luke 18:13.

[123]Cf. 1 Cor. 6:17: "But he who is joined to the Lord is one spirit."

[124]Cf. Col. 1:12: "Giving thanks to God the Father, who hath made us worthy to be partakers in the lot of the saints in light."

"And everlasting joy shall be upon their heads."[125] They are radiant, and their radiance constitutes their hymn to the One who is the cause of it. It is the "brightness of eternal light."[126] "Blessed are they that dwell in Thy house, O Lord; they shall praise Thee forever and ever,"[127] in that place of eternal praise. The Church, the Bride of Christ and the Spouse of the Holy Spirit, mother of souls and foster-mother of Christians, has filled its Offices with praise, and the prayer of joy before God is the form it normally takes.

[125]Isa. 35:10.
[126]Wisd. 7:26.
[127]Ps. 83:5 (RSV = Ps. 84:4).

Chapter 39

‿

Praise of man's powerlessness

All praise of God not commencing with an avowal of our impotence is less pure and certain. We must say to God, "My God, You are beyond anything I can imagine and beyond anything I can express. Between what I say to You and Your being there is and always will be an infinite abyss. For to praise is to know, and I truly know only one thing about You, and that is that I know You not. For that reason, I gather up all the power of my being in order to cry to You from the depths of my wretchedness, 'You are the greatness that exceeds all greatness.' " Such language alone is not altogether unworthy of God.

Our impotence need not, therefore, reduce us to silence. It forces us to express ourselves in two ways, which we can and must adopt according to the inspiration of the Holy Spirit. We can either make use of that speech which is beyond words, by endeavoring to reproduce the simplicity of the Word in the bosom of the Father who remains there in Him and completely one with Him, or we can have recourse to an endless multiplicity of ideas, of images and expressions of every kind, that try to reach the Infinite by means of the indefinite, calling on all creation to come to our aid and to join our poor hymn of praise to theirs.[128]

[128]Cf. Dan. 3:52 ff.

Chapter 40

⌒

Praise of God's goodness

My God, You are goodness in its essential source. You receive it from no one, and You possess it in possessing Your being. Indeed, it is Your being.

You are good in the same way as You are, and for as long as You are. From eternity to eternity You are good — eternally, immutably, infinitely. For You, to be and to be good are one and the same thing. Your goodness is Your being, and Your being is goodness itself.

All finite goodness comes from Your infinite goodness and is derived from it: a tiny rivulet, a mere drop. Our goodness is only what You make it; it is only insofar as it is connected with Your goodness, and it ceases to be when that connection is severed. All these finite examples of goodness attract me. I love them and would love to grasp them. I pursue them and exhaust myself in a pursuit which I know will more often than not come to nothing, and which, even when it does succeed, leaves me utterly empty and dissatisfied. And all the while I neglect the boundless Reality who alone can satisfy me and who is offering Himself to me.

Yet it is You I desire; it is You I seek under these many forms. I love them only because they reveal to me something of Your goodness, which is the only true goodness. You are the only One I truly desire and love, and the attraction of created things would cease if

The Prayer of the Presence of God

You ceased to be the One who is goodness itself and who gives Himself to us.

Goodness is the giving of oneself. Infinite goodness is the total gift of self, without limits, without reserve either in duration of time or space or in the giving of what one has and is. Goodness gives itself — like the sun shines, emits its rays, and diffuses its light; like a fire gives out its warmth or a spring pours forth its waters. You are that Goodness, that gift of self, that light, that heat, that spring watering the earth.

And You have introduced me into Your presence — me, a tiny thing: empty, cold, unknown, and self-centered — in order that I may receive, insofar as I can, Your being, which is all and wants to fill me to repletion.

༺

Chapter 41

Praise of God's wisdom

My God, you are infinite order. Now, such vestiges of Your order that we can find and perceive here below are marvelous and dazzle us — and we see so little!

You are so essentially "order" that even what we call disorder is made to serve Your designs. You possess the amazing power of making harmony out of dissonance. It is true: to recognize that supreme order, we must pass beyond the duration of time and present circumstances — in short, of what *is not* — and wait until the passing and superficial moment has produced what Your eternal gaze sees and Your immense love wills.

Your wisdom is this gaze, seeing far beyond time and distance. It emerges from a mind that creates order and a love that gives itself. The order is the outcome of the mind that loves, the proper name for which is Wisdom.

With men, the mind and the will, born of the same deep source, nonetheless seem divided. It would be more correct to say seem distinct, for distinction is not the same as division. In You, my God, in whom there is no division, they are one. Wisdom is the unique act by which You know Yourself in Your love, and love Yourself in that self-knowledge. Wisdom is Your Word, the light in whom You are revealed: the Word who expresses Your being, the Image who represents You, the substantial Ray who is the splendid brightness of Your glory,[129] the Likeness who reproduces Your features and makes You known.

This Wisdom has been communicated to "nothingness" and has filled it with finite reflections of HIM WHO IS. All beings, and the order in each of them, as in the whole of creation, makes known Your Wisdom, and it is there I must admire, adore, and love, when the world reveals itself to me in the splendors of its wonders and its harmony.

I must see in that splendor Your greatness, Your wisdom, and Your power — all the display of what I call Your perfections but which are in fact but the single perfection of Your plenitude of being. I must see in each, in the unity of each, a reflection of that infinite plenitude. I must see in all the elements composing it, and in all the ordered movements that constitute its activity, Your love unifying all, ordering all, reproducing itself in uniting, and uniting in ordering; and which, in order that all may act in consonance, arranges, preserves, and quietly develops the place and activity of each for the good of all, and of the whole to which each belongs.

This is the movement of which the Holy Spirit Himself speaks in the sacred Scriptures — this activity, masterly, measured, and in harmony, where all is accomplished smoothly and harmoniously and according to a plan foreseen down to its smallest details.[130] Its general and particular laws prove to be such a joy when we study them. They ensure our personal happiness and that of the world in general when we observe them ourselves, and they all tend to restore to everyone and everything something of that

[129]Heb. 1:3.

[130]Cf. Wisd. 8:1: "She [Wisdom] reacheth from end to end mightily and ordereth all things sweetly."

peace which reigns in Heaven. When the world allows itself to be governed by this Wisdom, it sees clearly without any kind of obstruction, since Wisdom is light. It is happy and makes light of the transitory sufferings of this life as though led by Your hand, for that hand is love. It shares Your light, which sees only love; Your love which wills only good; Your good, which is being itself. It re-enters Your unity, like the Word of whom it is the external expression, many-sided and fragmentary, yet unified by Him who is Wisdom ordering all things.

Your Wisdom shines in all creation as in Yourself — in the movement of the stars and of the seasons they affect; in the earth's vegetation governed by those seasons; in animate creation guided by so unerring and so wise an instinct; in intelligent beings that can err but can profit by their experiences, even when those experiences are at fault, in order to raise themselves higher and so come back to their Creator. It is reflected in the movements of pure spirits, whose intelligence (an intuitive movement) leaps upward to You in one bound and forever. They see what You see in the light of Your love, and they love all that You love. It shines in the movement of incarnate but distinctly spiritualized intelligences, by which even matter itself enters into that domain where You are always giving Yourself, and where everything has its abiding place. It shines in her who is the summit of creation, and in Him who is at the same time the head of all Your work and the Creator by whom all things have been made.

There I come back, with all I have described, to the essential Source where all was, before You gave the word for their creation; where all was accomplished when, with Your Incarnate Word and in Him, You made and consummated all things.[131] There I shall

---

[131]Cf. John 1:3: "All things were made by Him. . . ."

The Prayer of the Presence of God

eternally hymn this Wisdom, who is one with Your Life, one with You. There I shall see all, love all, and possess all. Seeing, I shall love, and my love will be light, and that love and light, together but always distinct, will proceed from Your being under my gaze.

Chapter 42

⌒

Praise of God's truth

However lofty they may be, all these words by their multiplicity make me always uneasy; they are so far from your unity. It troubles me to have to resign myself to my wretchedness as a creature, one who knows no other way of expressing himself. The angel in me protests; it would like to raise up the heavy weight of the beast which cannot dispense with them. But I am wrong.

Jesus has borne this weight; He raised it up and spiritualized it. He took it with Him to the serene heights of Heaven, to the eternal Father Himself. Having spoken of God's wisdom and of His Goodness, I can now speak of His Truth.

Your Truth, O my God, is that perfect unity reigning between You and the Word, who is Your expression when You tell Yourself inwardly what You are. For You speak, You see Yourself, and You know Yourself. You see Your being, who is light and love; Your interior communication (who is the Word) is the perfect expression of that perfect knowledge. You are light and love, and Your Word tells You that. He shows You that, in His blinding Light in Himself who, while coming from You remains one with You and returns to You. It would be truer to say that He never leaves You, but remains in the unity of the same Spirit. Facing You and receiving fully and clearly the infinite and infinitely limpid Image of Your being, Your Word reflects You fully, and gives back to You Your perfect Image.

The Prayer of the Presence of God

A perfect Image, He reproduces You wholly: there is complete
equality, perfect equation, between Him and You. And it is this
perfect and complete equality that is Your truth, child of Your love
and of the light of that love. You are that equality, and Your Word
is that equality; You are the truth because You are that equality.
You are the truth, and You express the truth in giving Yourself and
in reproducing Yourself such as You are; in producing that Image
who is all You are and does all You do. He is as You are, light and
love. He manifests Himself and, in so doing, gives Himself, just as
You give Yourself in manifesting Yourself.

Such, dear God, is Your truth. I believe it, although I do not
see it as yet. My words only express my faith, and they are uncertain and cold. But one day I shall see and I shall pronounce — I,
too — that Word, who is all light and love, because I shall be in
Him. Meanwhile, I am already partly in Him, since I believe in
Him. Every day God increases my faith, which always introduces
me more deeply in Him, that faith which is the clinging of my
being to His being, of my intelligence to His intelligence, of my
will to His will. It is this clinging that will make us one in the unity
of the Spirit.[132]

This truth is fully realized in You, my God, because You are the
infinite Spirit, who alone can give Himself wholly. Infinite Truth
comes from infinite Love, who in turn comes from the Truth and is
perfected in Him. Matter is purely on the surface and cannot give
itself; it can only be united superficially; its surface is all it has to
give. Spirit is wholly interior, and gives itself only interiorly. The
movement proper to it is interior, immanent, essentially total and
true. The Spirit thus gives Himself entirely and reproduces Himself

[132] 1 Cor. 6:17: "But he who is joined to the Lord is one
spirit."

entirely. Consequently, the Image equals the being who produces Him. The Truth of God is this equality, born of His love and of the gift of self, who is His movement and His life. Since God (who is being) is infinite, the Image also is infinite, for God gives Himself entirely. The equation is perfect, and that equation is truth.

All truth is in You, my God, for everything reproduces Your being, and all things exist in the measure in which they reproduce that being. My own truth and that of all things consists in this relationship. If I faithfully reproduce this truth, then I am in the truth; I am an image of infinite truth, in whose mind I already exist as an idea. There is an equation between this truth (the divine Image) and me and, through this Image, between myself and HIM WHO IS (that is, the Father). I must judge myself and all things, therefore, according to this relationship; my life depends upon it. If this relationship is exact, I participate in that Life who is the only true life — the life of HIM WHO IS. If that relationship strikes a false note, I am no longer in that being, in that life. Love, the participation in the Spirit of love, uniting the BEING WHO IS to His Image, the perfect harmony with this Image; the soul's delicate response to all the movements of this Spirit; its faithfulness in following His inspirations — this is the basis of my truth and my life.

My God, I am not sorry to have prolonged this meditation. It makes me realize that to gaze steadily at these truths is always rewarding. To dally with the purely superficial aspects of them leads nowhere, and the light it gives is barren. We have to dwell for a long time on these glimmers of truth; they become real only on that condition. Their life, like all life, is a synthesis; indeed the result of many syntheses, and it is all the richer since they are numerous and linked together. In a word, we must realize that being *is* unity; that unity is simplicity, simplicity is spirituality,

The Prayer of the Presence of God

spirituality is love, love is life, life is truth; and that all these realities (to which I give separate names because I know them only in
the broken mirror of Your works) in You are one — Your being, HE
WHO IS. And in that Truth, as in Your wisdom, Your life, Your
unity, it is HE WHO IS whom I praise with my uncertain song.

Chapter 43

⌒

Praise of God's mercy

I doubt if I can say enough of this on account of my wretchedness. I am a fallen angel! I have left the heights of being where You placed me when You created me. I did not know how to remain on that divine level, where I was truly in Your presence, in order to receive and reproduce the movement of Your Spirit, and recognize Him and His praise in all the created notes that reproduced Him without their knowing it. I had received the light that reveals this gift of self in everything, and the upsurge, conscious, awakened, and in full light, which makes it return to You. I have lost that light and have prevented that upsurge. I turned the light on myself instead of directing it toward You. I have deprived You of that glory and have wanted it for myself. I have reduced it to the measure of my own being, which is "nothing." And I have remained in that "nothingness," and all created things that I should have raised with me to You I have forced to remain there with me.

What a loss for us all! The consequences of Original Sin — and for that matter, of all sin — are terrible, if we only knew.

Our Lord knew this and bent beneath the weight of that knowledge. "My Father, if it be possible, let this chalice pass from me," He cried with His face bowed down to the ground and His whole body sweating blood, while His soul was sorrowful unto death.[133] He had descended to the terrible depths of my wretchedness and, by His Incarnation, used that very wretchedness to raise me up. To the abyss of my misery He opposed an abyss still more profound, that of His mercy. This latter is so deep that we meet God there, and find again our lost Paradise. Our very misery brings us back to God; it completes our movement and, without attempting to define that movement, I have the impression that nothing befits love more than mercy. To give Himself to our "nothingness" is beautiful and is a revelation of God's goodness, but to give Himself to our wretchedness is even better. To raise up calls for more love — is more the gift of self — than to create. The Redemption, the Blood of Jesus which flowed in our Lord's agony, at the flagellation, and on Calvary, is love's final word — if love can have a final word!

And You are that love; You are this culminating height, and it is there my life of praise must be spent.

Nor is creation excluded. I am still the voice of all Your creation, but it is at the foot of the Cross that I must sing my praise, joined by their voices united to mine and to that of the Son of Man, commending His soul into Your hands.[134] There all things are accomplished; all is consummated.[135]

God's mercy, as seen on Calvary, would seem to demand some kind of qualification, an epithet that does not exist. We need something to express — what, of course, is impossible — this God who dies. We must fathom the depths separating these two words *God* and *death*. We would like to have explained to us that death and all the circumstances to which He who died was willing to

---

[133]Matt. 26:38-39; Luke 22:44.
[134]Luke 23:46.
[135]John 19:30.

submit: simple "accidents" no doubt and more understandable than the being who died and the death of such a being, but nonetheless beyond our imagination. We would like to know all His capacity for feeling and consequently for suffering, with a body in which all, literally all, was broken, bruised, and crushed as in a winepress,[136] exacting the last drop of His Blood. But for that, we must know the soul that animated that body, the soul that felt the strokes the body bore.

But here, as always, the mind hesitates. . . . Endless perspectives of physical torture and moral martyrdom pass before my gaze and seem to challenge it, to dare my courage — or rather, my lack of courage — to gaze to the full. The saints have done it, and did nothing else. And at the end of their contemplation, they declared that they had not even crossed the threshold of that abyss.

From Calvary, God's mercy spread its waters over all men, at all times and in all places. It does so still and will continue to spread them until the end of time. But here still, here always, mystery confronts me, puzzles me, defies and overwhelms me. How is one to penetrate the marvels operated by grace in a single soul? The words of the psalmist come back to me: "He hath rejoiced as a giant to run the way."[137] The Redeemer is the giant who runs. I see Him set out, but the way escapes me. I only know that it is immense, that the mere idea of knowing it and following in His steps fills my heart with joy. And yet I must resign myself ever to confess my utter powerlessness, of which every meditation adds to my conviction and awakens my sorrow, were not even this sorrow a praise to the divine Majesty.

[136]Cf. Isa. 63:3: "I have trodden the winepress alone."
[137]Ps. 18:6 (RSV = Ps. 19:5).

The Prayer of the Presence of God

Fortunately, Holy Scripture is there with its words full of comforting light and consolation; its words telling me, almost all without my seeking, at least all I need to know. Perhaps one day I shall see it all more clearly; from that spring, which seems to me so deep, I might catch glimpses of those rivers that water the City of God.[138] For the moment, I recall just one, but one so intensely moving, that its syllables have always been to me like a mother's caress: "I have loved thee with an everlasting love; therefore have I drawn thee, taking pity on thee."[139]

How well You know, my God, to say these things; how delicate is Your touch. In You there is only love, and I still have not seen it clearly enough. Your mercy is but the reflection of Your love, when its light crosses the zone of the shadow cast by our sins. It is the movement of that light in the darkness.[140]

Our Lord, who is that light, came to enlighten that darkness. He, so to speak, left His kingdom in order to meet that darkness and there restore the radiant image of the Father. He came because He is love. He is the Son of the Father, who is love, and is that love's perfect ray.[141] From the Father He received that essential movement — the need to give Himself — and thus love gave birth, and is eternally giving birth, to mercy. That love, that mercy, needs to spread itself, to communicate itself, to radiate its brightness. It bears this need within itself, because it is born of the paternal bosom, whence this movement proceeds. The darkness, where that love and mercy do not shine, draws Him, appeals to this need, an appeal that seems to come from within it and says to

---

[138]Cf. Ps. 45:5 (RSV = Ps. 46:4). .

[139]Jer. 31:3.

[140]Cf. John 1:5.

[141]Cf. Wisd. 7:26: "The brightness of eternal light."

Him, "Come. . . ." And mercy cannot resist this appeal, since it corresponds perfectly to this need so essential to His being that He leaps and rejoices as a giant to run "the way."[142] He becomes the light who gives Himself to the darkness, and shines therein, becoming mercy, the love of HIM WHO IS for those who *are not*.

And to this nothingness He gives the power to give itself, even as He gives Himself — that is, freely and by love. This is man's privilege, his free choice. He can welcome that love or refuse it. If he responds, he becomes one with Him, and participates in His life and greatness. If he refuses, he remains in himself, in his nothingness, but in a nothingness shorn of all hope, a nothingness that could have been united to being, to God. It was called to be so united by grace, and was given the necessary powers. It could have enjoyed that union of love, but has failed to fulfill God's plan for it. As a result, it has been left a failure and a ruined thing. This is the real unhappiness that the divine mercy wants to succor.

[142]Cf. Ps. 18:6 (RSV = Ps. 19:5).

Chapter 44

Praise of God's justice

It is there, in the depths of our nothingness, that His mercy and
His justice — two things we do not usually associate with one
another — meet.[143]

In raising us up from the depths of our fallen state, God has re-
mitted our debt; He has restored His glory and repaired the dam-
age done by sin. He has truly resumed all His rights over us; He has
completely satisfied the demands of that glory; He has done Himself full justice. And we must learn to love that splendid glory and
to accept generously our wretchedness, which has procured it. We
must see, love, and praise His mercy and His justice, even in the
eternal punishments that do nothing to remit the debt. At first
sight, this mystery is terrifying; only after considering it long in a
spirit of faith does it become clear.

When faced with man's misery, mercy knows no limitation. If
that misery is not relieved, it is man's fault. It is he who refuses
Love's advances. To welcome those advances is the work of grace,
to which man's will responds. The rejection of grace is the work of
man's sole privilege, by which he is able to turn his back on God's
love. The all-merciful God has done all He can; He bent down to
His rebel son, spoke to His heart in order to touch and win it.

[143]Cf. Ps. 84:11 (RSV = Ps. 85:10).

Chapter 45

⌒

Praise of God's life

My God, You are the living God; You are Life. I do not know how to express this. I know it, but I cannot explain it. It is a truth beyond my understanding, still more beyond my words. The life of the spirit is a movement altogether interior. It comes from within, develops within, and is completed within. It is thus a spiritual movement.

Matter is not interior; it is all on the surface; it is not living. In order to live in it, the mind must in some way spiritualize it. The mind lives by its interior movement, which is its thought. Its thought is the expression of itself that it produces interiorly, and it is by this thought that it tells itself what is within it. It is like an image in a mirror. By gazing into the mirror, the mind produces that image, and it recognizes in it its being and the movement of that being which is its life.

I am always doing this, and it is the life of my spirit. I speak to myself, I express to myself what is in me. These are my thoughts, born of the union of my mind speaking to itself. They are not there already; they come from without. They are the result of a marriage. If my mind had only itself, it would remain sterile; it is the objects outside of it that render it fruitful. I can conceive what these objects are, because I enter into a relationship with them; it is they that have peopled the hearth of my mind with its numerous children. I live because I give birth to them, but I am not life, because the generative act is only partly interior.

But You, my God, You find within Yourself the object of Your thought. That object is Your being. You contemplate it eternally; You produce within You Your own image, who is Your Thought, Your interior Word, Your Son, the fruit of your union with Yourself. Eternally He receives that being, and eternally He reproduces it. He does what You do, for He is what You are. You give Yourself to Him, and He gives Himself to You. The "movement" that He produces is His movement because it is Yours. This is Your life — this interior movement passing from You to Your Image, giving birth to this latter, and going from Him to You. It is, as it were, a breath from Your bosom, yet remaining there, giving itself and revealing what You are by reproducing that being.

This movement is not like any other kind of life-movement that I know.[144] It is not the movement of a being; it is the movement of Life itself, or rather Himself, and that is why it *is* life. It is the movement of an ocean that has no shores. It is fed by no rivers. Nothing comes to it from outside; nothing goes out of its infinite being; the movement remains within itself. The swell of its tide

---

[144]The author frequently uses the word *movement* to designate the divine relations. He has explained elsewhere the sense in which he uses the word. "His movement," the author says, "is not our movement. I am in an entirely new world, where nothing begins, nothing continues or ends. . . . Our straight-track minds are at first at a loss. We think that to advance we must go from one point to another, and this is true where the starting-point is nothingness or complete indigence. But when the starting-point is Being Himself, the development can take place only within Him, by the communication of His being."

lights up the whole of its immensity; it is that immensity itself, and the movement of that immensity. [145]

Nevertheless, I distinguish in this immensity, in its unique movement and in the light that fills it, two terms. You look at Your Image, and Your Image looks at You; You are face-to-face. You take up this opposite (I would not say contrary) position, in order to see Yourself, to give Yourself, to be united and made one in the infinite unity which is the dream of infinite love. You are distinct, so that You can make but one, and You are infinitely distinct just as You are infinitely one. Hence the movement which is Your life and life itself. You move toward one another, one in the other, just as my mind moves in my thought and my thought in my mind. It is a movement like light in a mirror; like those who mutually love when they love with all the strength of their being. These are only comparisons far removed from the reality. They may give some idea of the unity, but not of the distinction. If they did, the unity they suggest would be endangered.

In finite beings, either the unity is imperfect, or those beings do not remain distinct. Only infinite being can be one and yet distinct. But here I am on the brink of a depthless mystery. I can penetrate it only with my eyes closed and with an adoring mind. Then You will give to these closed eyes a new light, which is the light of Your love, and which makes plain this mysterious life.

I see the being who gives Himself and the Image to whom He gives birth, looking at one another, enjoying one another, communicating one to the other that being who is all, happy in possessing and in giving. I see between the Source and the Image an

[145]Cf. Dom Augustin Guillerand, *Au seuil de l'abîme de Dieu: elevations sur l'évangile de Saint-Jean* (Rome: The Benedictines of St. Priscilla, 1961).

intimate relationship, which is this gift of self, this communication of the same being and in the same love. This is Your life.

This is Your life, such as my benumbed mind, my abstract thought, my lifeless words can represent and express it. It is Your life — and yet it is not! All I have said is but a very poor image, infinitely poor and meaningless, of Your life. Only faith can approach it, but on condition that it remains faith and not sight. I believe, and I am content. I no longer wish to try either to see or speak. I want simply to accustom myself to gaze into the shadows where the light is tempered so that I may not be blinded.[146]

You have not willed to keep to Yourself alone this communication uniting the three divine Persons in an infinite unity; You share it with us. It is that fountain of water "springing up into life everlasting."[147] Its waves penetrate the very depths of those souls that welcome the Holy Spirit, and vibrate to Love's every breath. It beats loudly at the closed gates of souls that remain deaf to it; it shatters at times those gates with its movement, which nothing can resist. Sometimes it waits a long while before letting loose its waters. Imperceptibly it glides across mountains, hills, and resisting rocks, the brushwood hiding its silent and scarcely perceived movement. It advances as best it can and forms its bed, at first narrow and contested but gradually enlarging itself until it is filled to the brim.

A strange mystery that I do my best to penetrate by these analogies. And yet the reality is truer, closer to myself and more intimate, than these realities to which I compare it, and yet I still have difficulty in understanding it, because I have compared it to material things, whereas it is wholly spiritual. Nevertheless, I begin to

[146]Cf. Isa. 64:4.
[147]John 4:14.

perceive it more and more by following it with the gaze of my soul, a gaze made more penetrating by a desire that is already an expression of my love, and which only infinite Love present in me has been able to excite.

The world is full of it. It is the burning light that shines and warms and gives birth to things; it is the sun, which pours down its rays and gives the light. We are there — like all creation lit up and animated by the physical sun — in face of that vivifying light of souls. We have only to open the windows of our soul, and that sun enters like a stream, its rays penetrating and lighting up, revealing everything in a new light. It is like the beginning of the dawn. All is covered with beauty; the youth of everything is renewed and, as it were, reborn. All the faithful in the world receive unceasingly its nameless benefit in the measure in which they want to receive it. All the company of Heaven and all the angels in Heaven are inundated and transformed by it. Its form becomes their form and their life. And with their whole being filled by it so that it is their act, their soul, and their full movement, they cry, "Praise to God in the highest."[148]

[148]Cf. Luke 2:14.

Chapter 46

⌒

Praise of all the divine perfections

Ought I not to have commenced with this . . . and have contented
myself with this gaze which, powerless as it is to describe and ana-
lyze this beauty so complete, yet admires its full perfection and offers its praise to the bouquet of all the perfections of which He
whom I adore is composed? But you, my God, are not even a bouquet; You are not composed. All perfections are in You, but they
form only one perfection, and it is to that perfection I offer my
praise.

You are the beauty who has made all beauty, and from whom all
created beauty comes. The beauty of created things is but a reflection of Your beauty in them. You are the divine Majesty and the
perfect loveliness; all that is noble and splendid; all that is rich
and powerful. You are the holiness and excellence of all that is
majestic and lovely, all that is noble and splendid, all that is powerful and rich, excellent and holy. You are the source of all these
perfections; they come from You; they return to You. They reveal
You to us; they draw us to You. They are the light by which we see,
or rather perceive, You. They are the voices that utter the numberless syllables of Your unique name. They are the rainbow hues of
Your infinite light. Their charm is but a distant expression, infinitely weak and remote, of the joy the actual vision has in store for
me. How true are the words of the prophet: "Eye hath not seen, O

The Prayer of the Presence of God

God, besides Thee, what things Thou hast prepared for them that wait for Thee."[149] The heart of man cannot have even a presentiment of that joy.

Nevertheless, what You have given of Yourself in Your works is very precious to me. They show You only as far, far away; they are only pale shadows of the reality, but they do reveal something of You; they make me think of You. What they lack tells me what You are not; their reality gives me some idea of what You are. Your shadow, which speaks to me through them, is a veil through which shines Your light, which is so beautiful. And if, in contemplating Your works, I do not know who You are, I know that *You are*, and I thank You for them, until I can sing Your praises with them in the true light hidden in them.

It is evident, then, that I must look beyond all matter with which Your works are made, beyond all limits of time and duration. You overflow time, which measures them, and space, which encloses them. You are eternal, immense, unchangeable. You are what these great words express, and even more what they do not express. You are greater than all these measures, than all my thoughts which are bound up with them. When I think of the accumulation of years and centuries without number, past and future, the idea of Your greatness that they give me bears no comparison with the reality. You are beyond all conception, beyond my dreams. That is why any words I use are negative, in that they say very little and indicate only what I cannot express, for Your reality is beyond all words and all thought. You are immense; that is to say, without measure. You are immutable; that is, without movement or change. You are infinite; that is, without limit, term, or frontier, without end. All I can do, then, is to put on one side all that is finite, all

[149]Isa. 64:4.

that is created and imperfect. I cannot express what is Your perfection. I merely indicate it vaguely by acknowledging my powerlessness to do so.

My language changes a little when I speak of Your perfections as seen in created things; such as when I speak of their intelligence, their will. Then I say, "God is intelligence, He is light; he is free, He is Love." But between this tiny light of intelligence that is in me and Your intelligence, the distance is such that even there my perception remains a vague and distant shadow. I dare not even think of it, much less describe it. We are on the same level, it is true, but I am at the opposite end. What I understand, compared with what You understand, is nothing. No created image can give any idea of what separates us, and once again I am reduced to confessing my nothingness, and making this my sole praise.

I would love to linger on the thought of Your will, which made all things with its single *Fiat!*[150] You made them freely, under no other pressure than the infinitely free pressure of Your love. I see You turned toward Yourself, occupied with Yourself alone, yet with all things in You. You are bound by nothing but Yourself, plunged in the infinite joy of giving Yourself to Yourself, and of pouring in the ocean of Your self-sufficient being all the riches of which it is the plenitude; of sharing them yet keeping them; of receiving them back even as You give them. This act is a single act, a single gift, a simple "willing" yet common to the three Persons, who act, love, give Themselves, and will all these things, and are happy in so willing.

[150]Cf. Gen. 1:6 ff.

⌒

Chapter 47

Praise of creation

And now I come back to our world, to our understanding of things, to our acts of the will — an attempt far, very far removed, to reproduce Your infinite intelligence and will. I see You as a sun enlightening all minds at all times, the source of all light for the mind. You are there (in the sight of these minds) in that inner chamber — where, having received and made them our own, we contemplate the images of things wherein your Spirit of light is reflected. I see them, only because You are there, within my mind and in the things themselves — within me, in order that I may find You in things, and in things so that You may increase in me (while I search them in Your own light). You are the Sun of Justice, the perfect equation, the fruit of love. You are the light giving Yourself in giving light to things, and revealing Yourself in giving Yourself. You are there in me, and by being there, You give me being. You make me see in manifesting Your presence and in revealing it as an eternal gift of self, in drawing me by that light to give myself as You give Yourself.

In this giving of Yourself to me in me, I understand something of the infinite gift of Yourself to Yourself in Yourself; of Your giving Yourself to every being in its being, according to a harmonious and varied scale, starting from the abyss and consummated in the Incarnate Word. I see all these beings reproducing Your being in

giving themselves and establishing themselves, at first unconsciously, then consciously in man, then in full consciousness and
light in the Incarnate Word. I see Your love snatching souls from
their nothingness in order to unite them to You, so that little by
little they may come back to You in giving themselves. I see Your
intelligence reproducing itself in this giving of self, directing it under the form of instinct, at first merely material but later living,
conscious, and gifted with reason, then fully awake and living in
Christ. I see Your love becoming light to manifest Yourself, so that
You may be seen from the moving of the waters of the abyss raised
up by the Holy Spirit, to the divine movement of Jesus on the
Cross, when He gave up His soul and with it all things to His Father,[151] from whom all things came.

I see the movement of this Spirit, the motive power of all being
and of all activity throughout the ages, and the light that reveals
this movement and inspires us to reproduce it. There is no uprais-
ing of the soul that does not come from that Spirit, no material
movement — not the movement of a rock or mountain, the
growth of a plant, the opening of a rose, the flight of a bird, the
hunting of animals in search of prey, the cry of an insect in a forest,
the glitter of sand in the desert or of a wave at sea, or the rays of the
sun in the air. You are there; You are responsible; You act; You are
the motive power, the guide, the rule and exemplar. And in the
other direction, in this "nothing" turned away from You in its refusal to obey You — the being implied in it still comes from you.
You are there. You not only praise Yourself, but You are both the
voice and the singer. The voice that comes from all creation and
loses itself in Your voice so that it may worthily praise You is still
Your voice.

[151]Cf. Luke 23:46.

I could continue thus for a long time. My thought could pass in review all places, all times, and the diversity of all creatures. I could consecrate my whole life to it. This is indeed what the sacred Scriptures do. I do it also when I recite the Offices of the Church: "Ye works of the Lord, bless the Lord. . . . Let the earth praise the Lord. . . . Praise Him, and give Him thanks."[152]

[152]Cf. Dan. 3:57, 74, 90.

⸎

Dom Augustin Guillerand
(1877-1945)

Born near Nevers, France, Dom Guillerand entered the Carthusian
Order at La Valsainte in Switzerland in September 1916, after his
ordination. In 1935, he was appointed Prior of Vedana in Italy and
convisitor of the Italian Province. In June 1940, forced to leave Italy, then involved in World War II, he found refuge at Carthusian
Motherhouse, the Grande Chartreuse, where he was immediately
appointed coadjutor to the Father General, and he held that post
until his death in April 1945.

Dom Guillerand was noted for his calm, peaceful demeanor, at-
tained by his long, continuous struggle to master his fiery nature.
This serenity shows through in his writings. Despite their richness, beauty, and wealth of spiritual insights, Dom Guillerand
thought little of his writings, and even destroyed most of them.
Fortunately a few of them, left to his nephew, have been preserved
and published for the benefit of today's readers.

Sophia Institute

Sophia Institute is a nonprofit institution that seeks to nurture the spiritual, moral, and cultural life of souls and to spread the Gospel of Christ in conformity with the authentic teachings of the Roman Catholic Church.

Sophia Institute Press fulfills this mission by offering translations, reprints, and new publications that afford readers a rich source of the enduring wisdom of mankind.

Sophia Institute also operates two popular online Catholic resources: CrisisMagazine.com and CatholicExchange.com.

Crisis Magazine provides insightful cultural analysis that arms readers with the arguments necessary for navigating the ideological and theological minefields of the day. *Catholic Exchange* provides world news from a Catholic perspective as well as daily devotionals and articles that will help you to grow in holiness and live a life consistent with the teachings of the Church.

In 2013, Sophia Institute launched Sophia Institute for Teachers to renew and rebuild Catholic culture through service to Catholic education. With the goal of nurturing the spiritual, moral, and cultural life of souls, and an abiding respect for the role and work of teachers, we strive to provide materials and programs that are at once enlightening to the mind and ennobling to the heart; faithful and complete, as well as useful and practical.

Sophia Institute gratefully recognizes the Solidarity Association for preserving and encouraging the growth of our apostolate over the course of many years. Without their generous and timely support, this book would not be in your hands.

www.SophiaInstitute.com
www.CatholicExchange.com
www.CrisisMagazine.com
www.SophiaInstituteforTeachers.org

Sophia Institute Press® is a registered trademark of Sophia Institute.
Sophia Institute is a tax-exempt institution as defined by the
Internal Revenue Code, Section 501(c)(3). Tax I.D. 22-2548708.